# WE OF LITTLE FAITH

# WE OF LITTLE FAITH

## Why I Stopped Pretending to Believe (And Maybe You Should Too)

## KATE COHEN

GODINE | BOSTON | 2023

Published in 2023 by
GODINE
Boston, Massachusetts

LIBRARY OF CONGRESS CATALOGING-IN-PUBLICATION DATA
Names: Cohen, Kate, author.
Title: We of little faith : an atheist comes clean (and why you should,
    too) / Kate Cohen.
Description: Boston : Godine, 2023. | Includes bibliographical references.
Identifiers: LCCN 2023002502 (print) | LCCN 2023002503 (ebook) | ISBN
    9781567927368 (hardcover) | ISBN 9781567927375 (ebook)
Subjects: LCSH: Atheism. | Irreligion.
Classification: LCC BL2747.3 .C615 2023 (print) | LCC BL2747.3 (ebook) |
    DDC 211/.8--dc23/eng/20230612
LC record available at https://lccn.loc.gov/2023002502
LC ebook record available at https://lccn.loc.gov/2023002503


First Printing, 2023
Printed in the United States of America

*For Noah, Jesse, and Lena,*
*my best teachers.*

# CONTENTS

# Prologue

## ACTUALLY AN ATHEIST

*I am going to bring floodwaters on the earth to destroy all life
under the heavens, every creature that has the breath of life in it.
Everything on earth will perish. But I will establish my covenant
with you, and you will enter the ark.*

GENESIS 6:17–18

IT WAS 2013. A mile-wide tornado had just ravaged Moore, Oklahoma—twenty-four dead, more than two hundred injured—and CNN had dispatched Wolf Blitzer to the scene. In front of splintered piles of metal and wood, under a blue sky, Blitzer interviewed Rebecca Vitsmun, a survivor whose house had been destroyed. He congratulated her on evacuating before the twister came, telling her that she, her husband, and her child were blessed. "You gotta thank the Lord, right?" he asked. Vitsmun paused. Blitzer pushed: "Do you thank the Lord for that split-second decision?"

"I'm actually an atheist," she said.

You can watch this clip on YouTube, and I'm sure I'm not the only atheist to have watched it more than once. It's thrilling. The assumption of religious belief upended! The glib reporter thrown off his game! The ritualized post-disaster piety popped like a balloon with one sharp-edged word!

But that one word was clearly hard for Vitsmun to say. "Do you thank the Lord . . . ?"—she paused, smiled, looked down, shrugged apologetically. "I—I—I'm," she chuckled, "I'm actually an atheist." She and Blitzer shared an uncomfortable laugh. And then she quickly reassured the television audience that she was still a nice person. "I don't blame anybody for thanking the Lord."

While it thrills me to see Vitsmun speak her truth, it saddens me to see her apologize for it. Apologizing is such a familiar reflex that, as I watch, I can feel my own shoulders do a "sorry" shrug. Like many women, I have been especially well trained to play along, to avoid saying "no" out of concern for other people's feelings. I don't live in Oklahoma—I live in Upstate New York—but still I have felt my own cheeks burn when saying the A-word. More often, I've chosen not to say it at all.

The comments following the clip include helpful after-the-fact advice on how Vitsmun *should* have responded, including snarky comebacks along the lines of "Yes, I thank the Lord he killed twenty-four of my neighbors and destroyed my home." But while it's nice to fantasize about thinking that fast or speaking that bravely—on camera no less—my own snappy retort would doubtless have gone something like this: "Do you thank the Lord . . . ?" "Um. We're so, so thankful to be safe."

It's surprisingly hard to stop a friendly conversation in its tracks. Which is why so many people who don't believe in God don't really talk about it, don't correct the false assumption, and don't call themselves atheists.

But Vitsmun did. She stammered out the truth about herself on national television. Despite the fact that, as I later read, her parents and coworkers didn't know she was an atheist. Despite the fact that, as she has said, she hadn't been planning to tell them.

It takes so little to tell the truth—and yet it clearly takes so much.

For Vitsmun, it took a tornado. It took being cornered on live television. And maybe it took one more thing, too, one small thing that's present in that moment: her child. During the entire interview, she's holding her toddler, the child whose life she just saved. The child she glances down at, right before she tells Blitzer the truth.

ᔆ

Americans who don't believe in God call themselves agnostics, humanists, skeptics, free-thinkers. They call themselves "spiritual." Sometimes they are called "nones"—from the box they checked on a survey identifying their religion. Sometimes they prefer not to label themselves at all. And sometimes they call themselves Jews. Or Catholics or Muslims or Buddhists. Rarely do they choose the word "atheist."

That used to be me. I was one of the many people who identify with a religion while disbelieving in the Supreme Being that lends it authority. I was raised Jewish and married a Jew in a Jewish wedding. As a child, a teen, even a young adult, though I didn't actually believe in that jealous, capricious, and cruel Old Testament God, I would not have called myself an atheist on a survey; I would have called myself a Jew. After I left home, I mostly steered clear of synagogue, but I kept my nonbelief to myself. I had lots of reasons to keep quiet, none of which were matters of life, death, imprisonment, or even disinheritance. (For example: Why would my metaphysical beliefs interest anyone else? Why make other people uncomfortable by expressing them?) Even as I began to believe that there might be some political significance in correctly labeling myself, I thought, why take a stand on *this* issue when so many others feel more urgent? I certainly wasn't going to risk having other people *not like me* just to set the record straight. Heavens!

Comedian and activist Sandi Toksvig has said that all people have an activation button inside them: the button that gets pressed when you think, *I must do something about this.* In her case, "this" was the fact that gay people did not have equal rights, including the right to marry, in the United Kingdom. The button "gets pressed for all sorts of reasons," she said. "My activation button was pressed when I had my kids."[1]

Mine too. Becoming a parent is a pivotal moment in many people's religious lives, but it's often one that brings them back to religion. Having drifted from the church or the synagogue after high school, having neglected if not outright rejected their own religious upbringing, many young parents return to it once it's their turn to bring up kids. Even if the idea of heaven once made them roll their eyes, heaven is the consolation they offer their children when burying the family cat.

For me, becoming a parent did the opposite. When it hit me that I was responsible for teaching my children *everything*, I knew in that moment that *I must do something about this*. And for me, "this" was the mindless transmission of information that I actually believed to be false, and "something" was telling the truth—to myself, to my kids, and, finally, to others.

I vowed to teach my children what I truly thought about everything, and that included what I thought about God: that like Zeus, Thor, Brahma, and Ra, he's a fictional character created to soothe the fears of ancient people. I would not—I did not—tell them that God *might* be real, just as I would not have told them the Mayan goddess Ixchel might be real. And if there's no supernatural being, then there's no supernatural place, either: tempting as it was, I did not offer my children the consolation of heaven when the cat died or when they themselves began to understand that their lives had a time limit.

All of this felt right in my head and in my home but radical in the context of the dominant culture. More radical still: I did not let them decide for themselves, as I would not with any other question of morality or the way the world worked. My insistence on telling my children what was true and what was fiction—my refusal to leave the question open—bothered even some of my nonbelieving friends. *Being* an atheist was one thing, but *raising* atheists was quite another, and far more questionable—at best, depriving children of the comforts of religion; at worst, brainwashing them.

I believe, to the contrary, that passing on one's preference for reason, evidence, and honesty—pointing out, with conviction and context, where fiction poses as fact—is the truly moral choice. It's one of the most powerful ways to stop the cycle of evasion and politeness that has given religious belief far more cultural, political, and legal power than it should have.

Most of us have grown up with this reflexive deference to religion, and many of us continue to act on it even if we don't ourselves believe in God. I still sometimes have to remind myself that it's okay not to tiptoe around religion as if it were a soufflé that could collapse and then the dinner party will be ruined. I'll never be totally free of that reflexive deference. But my children are.

❧

Although having children pushed *my* activation button, something else might push yours. A hypocritical Christian politician. A controlling in-law. The looming threat of an American theocracy. Another appeal to prayer after another gun massacre. A persuasive little book. *I must do something about this*, you might think. And what's the "something" you can do? You can be honest about being an atheist.

Many of us are not. Only 4 percent of Americans have told Pew researchers they identify as atheists.[2] But as many as three in ten said they were religiously unaffiliated,[3] and a 2022 Gallup poll found that only 81 percent believe in God.[4] It's easy to understand the numerical discrepancy in these data: there's a stigma attached to the absence or rejection of religious belief. Studies have shown that people don't trust atheists; they also don't want to vote for them,[5] and they don't want their children marrying them.[6] When pollsters come calling, it's easier for atheists to call themselves something else. Aware of this stigma and its potential effect on survey results, some researchers used a technique called "unmatched count" to estimate more accurately the prevalence of atheism in America. They found the actual number was more likely to be 26 percent.[7]

In other words, most atheists feel comfortable describing their beliefs . . . in other words. And that allows all of us to go on thinking, incorrectly, that atheists are a small minority of the American population, that belief in God is the norm, that only religious people are moral, and that biblical morality should rightfully exercise power over American law and politics.

Under the guise of religious liberty, "sincerely held religious belief" is increasingly being used to undermine the progress we have made as a country, from labor protections to health care to human rights. Many churches and synagogues fought emergency public-health regulations during the Covid-19 pandemic, for example, and the sincerely religious (as well as the sincerely opportunistic) argued for vaccine exemptions—no matter that the rules were in place to save lives.

Anyone's beliefs can lead to conflict with the law; why does a certain kind of belief give people legal immunity? Because: God. If a Supreme Being exists outside of human understanding, His capital-H authority supersedes the rule of law. That's why those who prefer His authority over, say, that of the US Department of Labor or the Centers for Disease Control and Prevention should get a pass (or so the "religious liberty" argument goes). Today, as Americans have finally begun to address and dispel the prejudices that religion cemented—if not invented—thousands of years ago, the religious right is re-staking its claim that religion should be the moral and legal driver of American life . . . a claim that is enabled by the well-intentioned religious left and by every single one of us who refuses to express publicly what we really believe: that God is a human invention.

Of course, although he is a human invention, he is one of our most durable. For many people religion offers deep comforts, and giving up God for good—along with the rules, regulations, and routines that spring from his authority—can feel like a loss. I understand that. I've felt that, too, despite being fully aware of the devastation that religion has wrought, including, as philosopher Daniel Dennett has put it, "bigotry, murderous fanaticism, oppression, cruelty, and enforced ignorance, to cite the obvious."[8]

I'm against all of that. But I don't want to focus on it in this book. I'm not interested in vanquishing religion or in convincing believers not to believe. I'm not even going to pretend I don't love singing "Amazing Grace" at top volume or filling my winter dining room with the light of Chanukah candles. I just want to change the default setting of American culture and politics from "In God We Trust" to "secular until proven otherwise." Together, I think, we can do that.

Raising children made it abundantly clear to me why people invented religion—why so many strays return to the pews after they have kids, and why even nonbelievers pass along to their children those religious beliefs (or half-beliefs, or the assumption that believing is the benevolent norm). Religion offers ready-made answers to our most difficult questions. It gives people ways to mark time, celebrate, and mourn. How should we think about death? How do we know right from wrong? How do we make sense of a world of wonders and horrors with no one in charge?

Those are questions I wrestled with as an atheist—and still do. My answers are not the only answers. They are probably not even my final answers. But they demonstrate that you can conduct a full life, a wonderful, even profound life, without relying on either the familiar religious structures or the supernatural beings that supposedly animate them. You don't need any special tools or training; you just need the determination not to pass on—by silent acquiescence or outright misrepresentation—what you don't believe to be true.

Six months after she declared herself an atheist on national television, Rebecca Vitsmun was interviewed about her heroic display of honesty. "I had this moment where I just stopped for a second and I realized, you either lie or tell the truth," she said. "And I, just, I'm not a liar."[9]

That's what this book is asking you to do: stop for a second, think about what you believe, and consider telling the truth.

# Part One

# THE MAKING OF AN ATHEIST

֍

*Religion, like a family estate, passes, with its encumbrances, from parents to children. Few men in the world would have a God, had not pains been taken in infancy to give them one.*

PAUL-HENRI THIRY, BARON D'HOLBACH,
*Good Sense without God*

# SHENANDOAH VALLEY JEW

*The Holy Land was as fabulous to me as the Land of Oz, and Jesus as mythical as Ali Baba. Only as figments of the imagination did I accept them, although I was willing to go along with this game that everyone seemed to be playing.*

RUTH HURMENCE GREEN,
*The Born Again Skeptic's Guide to the Bible*

I WAS RAISED REFORM Jewish in Broadway, Virginia, a small town in Rockingham County, the self-proclaimed "Turkey Capital of the World" (high school mascot: the Fighting Gobblers). We moved there when I was three, my father having been hired to teach at Madison College, in Harrisonburg, twelve miles south.

In rural, mostly Protestant Broadway, population around a thousand at the time, we were different, and being Jewish helped explain that difference. It explained why we didn't go to church and why we opted out of weekly religion classes at our public elementary school (or rather in a trailer just off school grounds, magically rendering them constitutional). Perhaps being Jewish explained other differences as well, like why we had dinner long after our neighbors had eaten and why our house was stuffed with books—although that could logically have followed from the fact that my father was an English professor. Maybe being Jewish explained that too.

Like any identity, our Jewishness helped explain me. And in a town where my sisters and I were the only Jewish kids, I sometimes had to explain *it*, to represent Judaism as if I were a diplomat from a small foreign country. My mom arrived at the elementary school every December, menorah in hand, to tell the Chanukah story. I often found myself insisting to astounded classmates that no, honestly, we didn't believe that Jesus was the son of God—not even a little.

Away from the public eye, my parents modeled a kind of bemused Jewish conformity, including a family rule about Shabbat dinner attendance that only my father was allowed to break. Shabbat is the Jewish sabbath, which lasts from sundown Friday to sundown Saturday. Officially, it is the holiest holiday, but the only part we took seriously was dinner. It was always the nicest meal of the week, preceded by the ritual lighting of the candles, after which we'd circulate around the table, murmuring "Good Shabbos" and kissing each person in turn, including our dinner guests whether they were Jewish or not. Most were not. But we'd graciously translate each prayer—over candles, wine, and bread—sometimes cheekily adding "and butter!" after the final blessing. A tradition, yes, but not a very pious one.

We belonged to the small synagogue in Harrisonburg, which we attended occasionally or never, depending on the oratorical skills of the presiding rabbi. There was high turnover. Our tiny congregation in the heart of the Shenandoah Valley didn't pay much, so we'd get young rabbis just starting out who would eventually leave us to move to a community that had, you know, Jews in it. I enjoyed going to "services" because I enjoyed family outings, dressing up, and singing. When the congregation was supposed to read aloud in unison, I made a game out of reading with all the feeling I imagined I should feel.

My sisters and I all became bat mitzvah. That is the grammatically accurate way to say it, because bat mitzvah means "daughter of the commandment," so it's something you become, not something you have. But in our family's idiom, we "had" bat mitzvahs and even "threw" bat mitzvahs because, for us, it was a party rather than a contract with the Jewish community or a promise to God. Chanukah was pleasant and jokey; Passover was long and food-y; Yom Kippur was a day off from school. Being Jewish meant being different and special in a way that totally conformed to (and doubt-less helped create) my self-image as an outsider.

It did not necessarily mean believing in God. At least not for me. As far as I can remember, I never believed that God was a real entity, a supernatural force with actual power, a being who listened to my prayers. He was a rich vein of philosophy and history and culture to be mined, a fascinating thing to think about. To me, the Old Testament God has almost too much personality to be persuasively "supreme." One of my children once complained about a food being "too tasty," and that's how I think about the Jewish God: He's petulant and needy, perverse and vengeful. He's prone to shifting shape and reversing course. He has a temper. In my Torah portion, the part I chanted in Hebrew to earn my bat mitzvah presents and the lavish attention of my guests, the Lord appears to Abraham as three men, whom Abraham hustles to welcome and feed. And then God, through these men (*as* these men?), tells the elderly Abraham and Sarah they will have a child.

> 12) So Sarah laughed to herself, saying, "After I have grown old, and my husband is old, shall I have pleasure?" 13) The Lord said to Abraham, "Why did Sarah laugh, and say, 'Shall I indeed bear a child, now that I am old?' 14) Is anything too wonderful for the Lord? I will return to you, in due season, and Sarah shall have a son." 15) But Sarah denied, saying, "I did not laugh"; for she was afraid. He said, "Oh yes, you did laugh." (Genesis 18:12–15)[1]

The drama! The menace! The Lord's very human response—I loved it. I was a reader, my whole family were readers, and my father taught Shakespeare for a living. To me, God was the same as any fascinating literary character, with one big difference: When we talked about Prince Hamlet or King Lear, we also talked about the playwright who created him, whereas when we talked about God, there was no explicit acknowledgment that an author was involved, that God was made up. I guess I assumed that's how my parents felt, and maybe they assumed that's how their children felt too. They never invoked God outside of ceremonial settings, never suggested we pray for anything, and never referred to Jewish law to keep their children in line. But, honestly, I never asked them if they believed in God, and no one—not my relatives visiting for Passover, my Sunday school teachers supervising the construction of sugar-cube models of the Second Temple, or the rabbis preparing me to become a Jewish adult—ever asked me.

# PASSING

*How much information does one person owe another?*
BROOKE KROEGER, *Passing*

A LTHOUGH AS A CHILD I may have felt like I was performing Jewishness, I didn't think of myself as faking it. I was a
Jew, simple as that, albeit not a devout one. I knew that Beth El
Congregation counted far more sincere believers in its fold, and
my Sunday school class certainly included children whose parents seemed to take the whole thing more seriously than mine.
But they were mostly children of professors or professionals,
too, in a predominantly Christian college town. We were, col-
lectively, what "Jewish" was, whatever slight distinctions there
were among us.

But when I got to college—I went to Dartmouth, in Hanover,
New Hampshire—the label didn't seem to fit as well. In some
ways, it would have made sense for me to cling to it even more,
since I felt out of place among the Lycra-clad blondes, the lacrosse
players, the boarding-school set. Yet devoid of its connection to
my beloved family and home, Judaism seemed suddenly alien and
strangely . . . religious. There must have been church services and
Christian clubs on campus, but I don't remember noticing them. I
do remember knowing where Hillel was, though, and seeing signs
for Shabbat dinners and High Holiday services. The students who
attended, it seemed to me, were Serious Jews. Observant Jews. The

kind who went on pilgrimages to Israel. The kind who abstained from eating bacon. That was not what I was.

But it was, during my senior year, what I pretended to be.

I had just returned from a spring term in Siena and a summer in Florence. I was living off campus, on financial aid, trying to get by on what I made from my work-study jobs. I thought I could keep my costs down by cooking in my little rental, but Dartmouth had changed the rules: you had to buy a meal plan whether you lived on campus or not. I couldn't afford to pay for meals I didn't eat, so I applied for an exemption from this rule based on the fact that (deep breath) . . . I wanted to keep kosher. With the righteousness of a privileged college student who wants every single goodie to which she feels entitled, I made my case to Dining Services. Dining Services said fine, as long as the college's rabbi in residence approved my request after an in-person interview. I have since repressed that nice man's name, but I can picture his nodding beard as I described my recent reconnection with my Jewish relatives in Florence and how that led inevitably to my wanting to keep my meat and dairy dishes separate.

In truth, I considered kosher laws to be outdated dietary recommendations that had been conflated with morality, and I felt (almost) no compunction pretending otherwise to save myself a few bucks. Only myself, mind you—if I had been truthful, I could have made my case against enforced college dining on grounds that would have done some good for other financially strapped students, and not just for me. But no. By faking religious commitment, I cheated the system for my own gain. I passed.

·◇·

Those Italian relatives had indeed made a big impression on me, though—that part was true. They had welcomed me to their Florentine homes while I was studying abroad and told me about their experiences after the enactment of the Leggi Razziali, Italy's antisemitic racial laws, in 1938, and the Nazi occupation of 1943. Rachel Neppi Modona, my grandfather's first cousin, had gone into hiding with her husband, Aldo, and their children, Lionella and Leo. It turned out that, during that period, the father and son of the family—Aldo and Leo—had kept diaries, which had never been published. So after college, I returned to Florence to conduct the research that would become my first book: translating those diaries (the authors had died) and interviewing the mother and daughter—Rachel and Lionella—about what it was like to hide from the Nazis.

I grew up some over the course of this research, and I began to understand better the logic behind the kosher laws I had so cynically exploited. In one of our interviews, Lionella, the daughter, described with loving pride how, when her family was in hiding and couldn't get kosher meat, the children would eat tref (non-kosher meat), but her father refused. He went hungry instead. And she told me with true sorrow how, at the end of his life, in the hospital, he was fed tref, unbeknownst to him. Fleetingly, in her sadness at her father's loss of autonomy, I glimpsed the logic of following these completely illogical rules. It was quixotic, it was self-defeating, but it was a way for him—a way for Jews—to preserve a sense of dignity and control amid the chaos.

I understood better, but I still acted poorly. Lionella and her mother, Rachel, were so generous with their materials and their time, and I assumed that their willingness to help was predicated on their sense of kinship with me. We were in fact literally kin, but because we were discussing a defining experience of their lives as Jewish people, it seemed important that I be Jewish too. Which I was, according to Mussolini's racial laws, but I certainly didn't feel it, didn't believe what they believed, didn't keep kosher or honor the sabbath or believe in God. Their Judaism existed in another universe, unfathomably far from my own family's winking participation or even from the rule-following of my boyfriend's—my future husband's—family. For the Neppi Modonas, Jewish observance was a pervasive and deeply felt element of everyday life.

I could have explained my true beliefs to them. Instead, I was careful not to reveal how I really felt about Judaism. At certain times, I even intimated a level of observance much higher than my own. And by "intimated," I mean misrepresented in a shamefully calculated manner. I didn't pretend I was just like them; that would have been suspicious. I calibrated my fake level of observance to a plausible degree. I would admit, ruefully, that no, my family didn't change all our plates for Passover or sell our chametz (the ritual purging from the house of anything with leavening, which is forbidden for the eight-day observance), but then reassure them that we certainly didn't eat the chametz we carelessly left lying around.

The truth was, when I was living at home, my family probably went through a couple of boxes of matzo over the course of the week, if you added up school sandwiches, matzo-and-butter snacks, and my father's singularly greasy fried matzo. Did we avoid Cheerios for eight days? No, we did not. Were all the other boxed and processed foods we ate that week stamped kosher for Passover? No, they were not. Did we take the whole thing seriously? Only as far as taking it seriously was fun.

Most of my attempts to pass as a believer in the Neppi Modonas' presence—like most people's attempts to pass as Christian or straight or whatever the favored identity might be—didn't involve outright lying. They involved keeping my mouth shut. Not questioning customs. Not venturing my own views on the State of Israel. Smiling sheepishly when scolded for writing a letter on a Saturday morning.

While carrying out this low-key but near-constant deception, I was simultaneously learning the story of how my relatives avoided deportation and death after the Nazis invaded Italy in 1943 by hiding in the hills near Florence and pretending to be Catholics. The following is a snippet of an interview I conducted with Rachel about her deceased son.

RACHEL

But Leo always said, "Mamma, you have always taught us that one should never tell a lie, but now we're always telling lies."

ME

And what did you say? How did you explain?

RACHEL

We explained to him, they are lies to save ourselves, that's what we said.[1]

Meanwhile I, at that moment (more or less), was lying to save . . . face. To save my relationship with this family. To save my project. My cousin and I both fell somewhere on a crowded continuum of people who pretend to be something they are not, motivated by everything from financial gain to courtesy to defending their family from a murderous regime.

We had something else in common, too, I suspect. Lionella, the daughter, told me that she and her brother were extremely ill-prepared to pose as Catholics: they never learned any prayers, she always got the sign of the cross wrong, and her parents "came up with such terrible [fake] names!" (Her future husband, who was also in hiding and pretending to be Catholic, had by contrast learned to serve Mass.) So badly did they fake it, according to Lionella, that she ultimately came to believe that everyone in the village had known or guessed the truth, and that her family's safety was guaranteed not by their skills at dissembling but by the parish priest, who made a point of walking across the whole town with his hand on her brother's shoulder. The Neppi Modonas pretended to be Catholic like their neighbors, and their neighbors pretended to believe it. Likewise, I'm pretty sure Lionella could see through my wily attempts to seem more religious than I was. She was sharp-eyed, critical, and thoughtful; that's why I loved to interview her and why I was afraid to let her down by being honest. But it's also why I believe we participated in a kind of "pass" *de deux*, in which I played a part and she played along.

ᴥ

One of the conclusions I came to while writing *The Neppi Modona Diaries* was how little I identified with the worldview and belief system of those deeply religious women—that is, how *not* Jewish I felt. I noticed that any time I tried to imagine myself living in Florence when Mussolini began to incite antisemitic sentiment— when I asked myself whether I would have understood what was happening or how I would have behaved—I pictured myself not in their situation, as a persecuted Jew, but as a bystander. Living with and learning about the Neppi Modonas both revealed and widened the distance between my identity and my beliefs.

Nevertheless, a few years later, back home in Virginia, I married my college sweetheart, Adam, in a Jewish wedding. Though neither of us were believers, we were both raised Jewish, so for us a Jewish wedding was the path of least resentments. It would vaguely please my parents, who probably didn't care much themselves but wanted to please *their* relatives. And, on the other side, it was essential for keeping Adam's father from completely losing his shit. My soon- to-be father-in-law kept kosher, attended an Orthodox synagogue, and had subjected Adam and his siblings to a Jewish education as rigid as mine had been relaxed. But as long as there was a rabbi, a huppah (traditional wedding canopy), a smashed glass, and a smat- tering of Hebrew, we figured he could ignore any . . . irregularities.

We had to import the rabbi (small-town Virginia, remember), and through a family friend we found a hip, progressive one—a left- ist intellectual from George Washington University. We explained to him that we weren't very religious and that we'd rather not talk a lot about God if we could help it. We then wrote God out of the entire ceremony except for a single obligatory line of Hebrew.

But it was a Jewish wedding! If you'd been there, you might well have gotten the impression that we took seriously the faith of our forefathers. It wasn't a ruse—it was more complicated than that—but it wasn't the truth, either. I never said I was an atheist and neither did my husband. And neither did the rabbi, although he could have been. So, yes, we placated my father-in-law lest he make life unpleasant for us, given that we were and would continue to be living on the family farm down the road from his house. And, to be honest, lest he retract my beloved-daughter-in-law status. He didn't really know me, but he did love me to the best of his ability, and I needed him to. I needed pretty much everyone to at the time, but especially him, with whom our future was entwined. I wasn't willing to take any great risks or make any grand statements that might alter his idea of who I was. I chose instead to play "Kate"—a young Jewish woman in a white dress listening earnestly to the rabbi under the huppah. He perfectly looked his part, with his glasses and authoritative beard. We looked our part too. There was some hesitation about whether Adam would wear a yarmulke, but at the last moment, right before the ceremony began, he slapped one on like a small, round white flag.

# AN ATHEIST IS BORN

*To be a kid requires difficult detective work. You have to piece*
*together the entire universe from scratch.*

KAREN RUSSELL, "The Ghost Birds"

THREE YEARS AFTER OUR wedding, we had our first child.
Then another after two years. Then, after a bit of dithering,
a third.

In the usual story, this would be when your formerly unobservant Jew—newly married, newly a parent, making a home and a
family far from where she grew up—starts shopping for a synagogue. Having kids often brings people back to their childhood
religions, to the familiar one-stop shop for community, values, and
answers to life's Big Questions. But for me it was the opposite.

Having children made me an atheist.

You already know I wasn't a true believer. I didn't have a personal God to reject. It was not a matter of shaking my fist at a heedless
sky while stumbling out of bed for the third time in a night. Or
shaking my head at the cosmic injustice of bearing kids who wanted for nothing while countless others were born into a lifetime of
want. This epiphany was about newfound clarity and conviction.
Having kids forced me to understand and articulate what I really,
deep down, believed to be true.

Why? Because I couldn't lie to them. I was a little compulsive
about this throughout their childhoods. My husband was fully capable of changing the clocks in the middle of the night in an at-

tempt to get an extra hour of sleep once in a while; I couldn't even pretend, when advertising dinner, that orzo was rice. It's not that I thought kids were so pure that they should be protected from the creeping contagion of dishonesty, or that I wanted to set a good and moral example, or even that I believed lying is always wrong. I didn't.

But I did feel obligated to help my children understand the world as it actually was. Why would I make my job harder in the future by misleading them now? Why would anyone? Once you tell your children that babies are delivered by storks or Christmas presents by Santa, at some point you will have to *un*tell them. I guess you could figure they'll learn it on their own, but then they would trust you less. By lying to them, even about silly things, I would be both burdening my future self with the issuance of corrections and undermining my own credibility. The sooner they learned that they sometimes had to eat unfamiliar foods, that they sometimes had to be quiet in the morning because Mommy and Daddy had too many martinis last night, and so on, the better. So when our cat died, I stopped myself from saying that he had gone to sleep, gone to live on someone else's farm, or gone to heaven. At some point they were going to learn that the cat was dead, and dead meant gone forever. If they learned it from me, I could help them try to make sense of that strange, sad, perspective-shifting fact. Helping them understand their world, plus feeding them, was essentially the whole job.

When I had children, I felt the awesome responsibility of being a portal to every single thing they knew about the world. I could not imagine teaching them something I didn't know to be true. Or telling them something I knew wasn't true.

When I had children—or, more precisely, when I started teaching them things—I realized that our lives and our heads are full of half-considered actions and half-digested philosophies and entirely unproven received "wisdom." I knew I couldn't undo most of this mess in my own head, but, now that I was given a fresh start in the form of unformed humans, I could at least try not to pass it on to them.

Every nugget of conventional wisdom that popped into my head had to pass the truth test before I was willing to pass it along. Sometimes the kids would bring a truism home from school for my inspection, so I'd have to say things like, "Of course you should talk to strangers! How else are you going to meet people?" Not lying—and not passing along half-truths—also meant examining what I really thought about things, what I really believed. Since I wasn't going to pretend that the chicken we were eating for dinner was anything other than a *chicken* like the one they saw in their picture books, I'd better be able to explain why we ate animals—or stop eating animals.

"We don't eat pepperoni," a friend of mine once said to her three-year-old son, shooing him from the pizza box. "Why?" he asked. She thought. She answered, "Mommy and Isaac don't eat pepperoni. It's spicy. Mommy and Isaac don't eat pepperoni because it's too spicy." Um, that's not why. If it's because pork isn't kosher, why doesn't she just say, "Because pork is unclean"? Or "Because God says it's wrong"? Maybe . . . because my friend doesn't really believe any of that? Or she's not sure what she believes, but she's not eating pork until she figures it out? Or she's not eating pork to remind her of her childhood of not eating pork? Or to keep that "I'm Jewish" feeling going, despite the absence of synagogue or home ritual or even—possibly—belief?

You don't have to understand something completely, or rid yourself of all ambivalence, to start answering honestly. You can just start and see what happens. You can tell your child, "Pepperoni is made of pig, and a long time ago there was a rule that Jewish people don't eat pig, and Mommy wants us to follow that rule."

At which point the kid will say, "Why?" So you keep going: "Following the rule makes Mommy feel connected to other Jewish people and also to her parents and their parents. And that's why she wants you to follow the rule, too, so you can also feel connected."

By now the kid has wandered off, bored. Job done. Sure, he doesn't understand. He's three! But you haven't lied, or put off answering honestly, or gone on record as opposing spicy foods. You may have even started to think about your own choices more clearly than you have before.

That's why I loved the "why" years. I recommend that everyone spend time in the company of an inquisitive child. If you don't have one, borrow one—I promise you, your friends with kids are generous lenders—or failing that, try installing an imaginary one in some corner of your brain to help you filter out all the crud you don't actually believe.

One admission: My determination to tell my children the truth when they asked me a question (or even when they didn't) wasn't just an intellectual stance I took based on my understanding of the responsibilities of parenthood. It was also, for me, an emotional imperative. When I was a child, I would feel physically ill upon discovering a disconnect between what I had thought and what turned out to be true. I hated to be fooled, misled, deceived, or even persistently mistaken. More precisely, I hated to discover that I had been duped, to cross that dividing line between ignorance and understanding and look back across time at my painfully innocent self. As an adult, I couldn't bear the idea of causing that feeling in someone else. Even briefly. Even in fun.

When I was twenty, I went to visit my aunt and her little girl. Another cousin who was about my age happened to be visiting too. When I arrived, he was cracking himself up over a game of hide-and-seek in which the toddler kept finding him on the sofa in the living room, while he kept insisting to her with a straight face that he was actually in the kitchen. She looked doubtful, but then left the living room to go looking for him, at which point he collapsed in giggles. A harmless game, of course, poking fun not at this girl but at this stage of human development. But it made me feel sick. Her trust and vulnerability and lack of understanding, his amusement.

Fifteen years later, there was no way I was pretending to be the Tooth Fairy. Here's my child struggling to understand the world, trying to fit all the pieces together, and I make his job exponentially more difficult by throwing in a fiction that I pretend is a fact? And then my kid has to worry about how the Tooth Fairy gets into the room or whether she can find his tooth, or what will happen if he's away from home when the tooth falls out? And eventually the kid has to deal with the growing suspicion that the Tooth Fairy doesn't exist after all? That everyone else might know the truth, but he doesn't? No—stop—I can't!

These are the circumstances under which, in our house, God didn't stand a chance.

I didn't set out to call myself an atheist or raise atheists. To me, it was this simple: I believed that gods were fascinating characters and sometimes useful fictions employed by people around the world and across time to explain their place in the universe. That, I resolved, was what I would teach my kids.

# THUNDERBOLT

*The religion of one age is the literary entertainment of the next.*
RALPH WALDO EMERSON, "Character"

I CAN TELL YOU the exact moment when I started to raise my children as atheists. It didn't feel momentous at the time, but it was a moment. Noah was five, Jesse was three, and we were sitting on the couch reading from *D'Aulaires' Book of Greek Myths*, a holdover from my childhood bookshelf. Those illustrations freaked me out as a kid; it's one thing to *read* that Cronus ate his babies, but it's quite another to *see* it. So naturally I had to share the experience with my boys. Sure, parenting is about helping your children navigate the world, but it's *also* about facing your demons while protected by total adoration and small warm bodies clad in footie pajamas.

Anyway, one of the boys asked what a "myth" was, and I told them it was a story about how the world works. People used to believe that these gods were in charge of what happened on Earth, and these stories helped explain things they didn't understand, like winter or stars or thunder. "See: look"—I flipped ahead to find a picture—"Zeus has a thunderbolt."

"They don't believe them anymore?" No, I said. That's why they call it "myth"; when people still believe it, they call it "religion." Like the stories about God and Moses that we read at Passover or the ones about Jesus and Christmas. They're just made-up stories, like myths, but people still believe them.

Here's how the D'Aulaires' book begins:

> In olden times, when men still worshiped ugly idols, there lived in the land of Greece a folk of shepherds and herdsmen who cherished light and beauty. They did not worship dark idols like their neighbors, but created instead their own beautiful, radiant gods.[1]

"Every people creates its own gods," I said. The little warm bodies nodded, and we proceeded to Gaia and the Titans, until I could feel Cronus lurking behind the next page.

That was it: the big moment. I didn't set out to raise atheists per se. Before I had children, I certainly never planned to tell my children that religions were made up. I planned to read to them all the time and feed them food I made myself and make sure they wrote thank-you notes. That was about it, except for one more thing: I planned to tell them the truth.

# THE TRUTH, THE PARTIAL TRUTH, AND NOTHING LIKE THE TRUTH

*A subject is raised which the liar wishes buried. She has to go*
*downstairs, her parking meter will have run out. Or, there is a*
*telephone call she ought to have made an hour ago.*

ADRIENNE RICH,
"Women and Honor: Some Notes on Lying"

EXPLAINING TO MY CHILDREN the difference between a myth and a religion was pretty much how I had talked to them ever since my first was born—constantly, and with far more explanation than they needed. It began not with a discussion of metaphysics but with mundane maternal chatter. I talked to them nonstop, telling them everything I believed to be true, tasting each statement for toxicity and nutritional value before passing it along. I wouldn't just say "tree"; I would say "maple tree" (after checking to make sure it was). I declined to refer to close friends as "Aunt Betsy" or "Uncle Mike" because they weren't technically my children's aunts and uncles, and I let Noah call me Kate because I couldn't think of a good reason why he shouldn't call me what everyone else did.

Eventually he started calling me Mom, and I was glad—partly because I felt I'd earned the title, but also because it clearly bugged other people when he didn't. I still cared what other people thought. I was still willing to misrepresent myself rather than risk disapproval. So while inside our home I was a scrupulous truth-teller, outside I was decidedly not.

I had little kids, so I had to leave the house sometimes to save my sanity. When Noah was just under one, we signed up for a

Mommy & Me class at a nearby synagogue. Two mornings a week, we (mostly) mothers gathered to learn how to do the hand motions for "Itsy Bitsy Spider," brought snacks we thought expressed the right level of casual healthfulness, feigned interest in other people's children, and remembered how to have adult conversations. And there, among the mommies, I was less than forthcoming about me.

"Are you guys affiliated?" they would ask (meaning, "Are you members of a synagogue?"). I would say no—that was true. But it was true in the way that a lesbian might say no when someone asks if she has a boyfriend. It was true but it wasn't *the truth*; it left the door open for them to think I was something I wasn't. Even if I did not belong to a synagogue, you see, I could still be a believer. Theoretically, I could be *so* devout that I hadn't yet found a religious home that met my doctrinal specifications.

Or they would ask, "Are you Jewish?" And depending on my split-second assessments of their preferences in such matters, I would answer, "Yes." Or "Yes, culturally speaking." Or "Yes, but not very religious." Or "Sort of."

Venturing a "We're not very religious" was easy, at least where I lived. "We're just in it for the food": ha ha. But "No, we're atheists"? That felt like too much information, the kind that invited an awkward pause. The kind that stopped conversation, when conversation was what I craved.

At home I had taken a sort of parental vow of honesty, but out in the rest of the world . . . well, I wasn't everyone's mom, was I? And yet, the more I had to explain things to my children, from death to Christmas carols, the more I realized that "atheist" was what I was. What we were. And the more firmly that label lodged in my head, the more I felt like I was constantly, actively hiding it from everyone. Childhood friends who didn't know the grown-up me. Distant relatives I saw every few years. Jewish elders I admired. A Catholic mom with an infectious laugh. A dear friend's devoutly Christian girlfriend. Someone would ask what we were doing for the holidays or whether the boys had started Hebrew school or even the seemingly innocuous question, "Have your boys thought about joining the Boy Scouts?" I said no to the Scouts and, when pressed ("It's great! Your boys would love it!"), I begged off on account of their policies on homosexuality, which was more than reason enough in my view. But it was also only half of the real answer, which is that the Boy Scouts also didn't allow atheists. (At that time, a Cub could earn not one but two prejudice badges.)

Round and round the circle of moms at Mommy & Me or the Little League game, innocuous question after friendly overture after the Pledge of Allegiance. Duck . . . duck . . . chicken.

I lived in the Northeast. I was self-employed. My family knew I wasn't a believer. What was I afraid of? I was afraid some people wouldn't like me. I was afraid they would judge me or think I was judging them. I was afraid of having an awkward conversation.

So I didn't. It was easy. People do it all the time: we let things pass. We answer questions we weren't asked to avoid the answers we're afraid to give. We say what we must to fill the space where truth would be if we could bring ourselves to say it. "I've got to read up on the candidates" [truth: Democrats down the line]. "We don't talk much" [she cut me off completely]. "People really love that show" [I just lost all respect for you]. "Oh, us? Jewish" [atheist].

Even after I started writing about being an atheist, I found myself tongue-tied in person when people asked me, "What do you write?" or "What are you working on?" I was—I still am—far braver in print, and saying out loud that I was an atheist felt like it required a level of bravery that was beyond me. I couldn't, for instance, tell Joanna, a woman I'd met at our boys' preschool. Joanna was funny and warm and unflappable; she could not be flapped. She told entertaining stories about her kids but never bragged, she loved her kids but didn't dote, and she let her son wear a tutu to preschool. The cross pendant she wore gave me pause—I didn't think it meant something bad about her, I just thought that maybe we were too different—but in the end, Joanna was irresistible. We made the leap from school hallway chats to home get-togethers, and one evening Joanna asked me, from across her kitchen counter, what I was writing these days. I froze. What I was writing was an essay on being an atheist. And then I took a deep breath and . . . told her about an architecture book I was ghostwriting. The conversation moved along—school sports, town politics, pink tutus—but my cowardice weighed on and distracted me. Why couldn't I tell the truth? Did I think she wouldn't like me anymore? Did I think she would think I thought less of her, since she was evidently (or at least ornamentally) a Christian?

Can you be a real friend of someone with whom you won't be honest?

·◌·

I realize I have just breezily confessed to years of lying. The wary reader might well wonder just how much I can be trusted. And the astute reader might find it difficult to square my assertion that I couldn't lie to my children with my history of deceiving pretty much everyone else.

So let's talk about lying for a minute.

I like the definition Sam Harris uses in his book *Lying*: "believing one thing while intending to communicate another."[1] Harris believes that lying is nearly always bad. To him, the casual dissembling that most of us think of as kindness is actually cruel. To him, "Yes, that dress *does* make you look fat" and "No, I don't think you have what it takes to be an actor" are acceptable statements, and in fact they are morally preferable to letting a friend persist in delusional and (to his mind) harmful behaviors, such as failing to lose weight or clinging to the doomed dream of an acting career.

My attitude toward lying is more practical and less dogmatic. I think it's a useful, sometimes essential tool for the powerless to use against the powerful. Parents often get upset when their children lie to them, but lying is in fact a totally rational response to the totalitarian regime under which children live. Parents make all the rules and hold all the power. They give and they take at will; they praise and they punish as they see fit. The only thing a child really controls is the space between his brain and his mouth.

When my children lied to me, I saw their lies as barricades they had erected to protect their true selves from my prying. I didn't see lying itself as a crime that required punishment, and I didn't get angry. I just tried to work around the barricades, focusing instead on whatever I was trying to accomplish that they were trying to resist. Sometimes that meant implying or outright stating that I knew they were lying. "Well, dear, nice try. Obviously, you didn't actually practice because your brother's sheet music is out on the piano, not yours." Or: "Hmmm, you *say* you practiced but I didn't hear it and neither did your dad, so I'm afraid you'll have to practice again, louder this time."

Although I accepted that my children lied and understood why they did, I still didn't like it. I didn't like being denied access to their reality—what they truly felt, thought, or did. They did something with that half hour of not-practicing, and the knowledge of what they did existed inside their heads, where I was not permitted entry. They were keeping me out. That's what private lies do, from false praise to fictitious scheduling conflicts to fake orgasms. Lies create barriers between people. Sometimes you need that. Sometimes you'd be better off without.

When I lied to my Italian relatives, to my college, and to assorted fellow moms about my beliefs, I was protecting myself, and sometimes I may even have thought I was protecting them. I lied to avoid conflict, hurt, suspicion, cafeteria food, awkwardness. But in doing so I may also have been avoiding great conversation, intergenerational understanding, institutional progress, and deep friendships.

My cousin Lionella and I could have been close, I think; instead, after I finished the book about her family's experiences, we maintained a warm but not intimate correspondence. And the irresistible Joanna and I never see each other anymore. Maybe all we suffered was normal suburban family drift: after preschool our kids went to different schools, and life is busy. But I still wonder sometimes what might have happened if I had told her the truth.

# THE HALLOWEEN PARADE OF 2006

*The more false we destroy the more room there will be for the true.*
ROBERT G. INGERSOLL, "Orthodoxy"

T HE FIRST TIME I told someone outside my family circle
that I was an atheist was in Mrs. O'Brien's first-grade classroom on the biggest holiday of the elementary school calendar:
Halloween. The room had been transformed by cotton cobwebs,
cardboard witches, and black-and-orange streamers. Parents sat on
child-size plastic chairs to watch the costume parade, and I was
grateful for the perch, having just spent several frantic hours in
my kitchen affixing fruit-leather fingernails to sugar-cookie fingers. They looked amazing until I placed them on the buffet with
all the other themed foods (marshmallow ghosts, spiders made of
gumdrops and licorice), and then they looked like something that
would get thrown away the moment the school day ended.

Sitting next to me was Julie, a slender brunette in a charcoal
pantsuit and heels; she had come from work. We chatted as we
waited for each child to get into position and receive applause. Harry Potter, Anakin, Batman, Disney princess, witch. *That's mine over
there.* Harry Potter, Anakin, Spiderman, Disney princess, ghost.
*There's mine.* My second child had just turned four, and the conversation turned to preschools. Julie mentioned a well-regarded
program in a synagogue—had we visited that one? I paused before
I answered. We had, in fact, visited that one, but we had crossed

it off the list because it was too religious. The kids were not just making menorahs out of egg cartons and eating challah for snack on Fridays but actually learning prayers by heart. *Far* too religious. Should I tell her that? I was emboldened by her cosmopolitan look, her manicure. She was clearly smart: what she had brought to the Halloween buffet was the napkins.

It was the perfect opportunity for me to push myself toward honesty. I was never going to bring it up out of the blue. I still wanted to be . . . appropriate. I wasn't about to respond to "Gorgeous day, isn't it?" with "God has nothing to do with it." That would be obnoxious. "And how do you know the bride?" "Well, I certainly didn't meet her at church, since I'm an atheist." Not believing in God was neither all I did with my day nor the only subject on my mind.

It would be plenty just to give the true answer, the complete true answer, to an actual question. At the Halloween Parade of 2006, that question was, "Why not the Ohav Shalom nursery school?" The answer was that I didn't want my child spending a significant portion of his week learning prayers to a God I didn't believe in.

Harry Potter, Anakin, Spiderman, Disney princess.

Maybe what finally made me take a chance that day was sheer boredom. Telling the truth and risking a stranger's disapproval was like biting the inside of my cheek to keep myself from nodding off.

"It was too religious for us," I told her. "We were raised Jewish," I plunged on—can a person both speak and hold her breath?—"but we don't believe in God or anything."

"You mean you're atheists?" I nodded. She marveled: "I've never met an atheist before!"

Her manner was a combination of curious and awed. I exhaled. But: really? Never met an atheist before? Of course I wasn't the first atheist this educated, professional woman had ever met. She had been to college; she worked in downtown Albany. I pictured a gay teenager coming out to her aunt. "I've never met a homosexual before!" *But Auntie, you live in New York City!*

Even people who are aware that some people don't believe in God often assume that everyone around them does. I wasn't the first atheist she'd encountered; I was the first who admitted to it. And, sadly, my revelation was just that—an admission, not a declaration. Perhaps you noticed that I let her say the scary word for me. I said, "We don't believe in God *or anything*"—"or anything" was the conversational equivalent of "move along, folks, nothing to see here." She's the one who said "atheist."

# WHY I DON'T CALL MYSELF
# AN AGNOSTIC

*I'm an atheist, and that's it. I believe there's nothing we can know
except that we should be kind to each other and do what we can for
other people.*

KATHARINE HEPBURN

L ET'S FACE IT. "ATHEIST" can be a hard word to say. It
sounds so definite, so absolute, so final. So why don't I just
call myself an agnostic?

After my meek admission to a fellow spectator at the first-grade
Halloween parade, everything returned to normal. As far as I can
remember, Julie told me about her conversion to Judaism and her
children's religious education. I told her about my upbringing and
my Jewish wedding. And then we discussed . . . the reemergence of
Star Wars characters in the Halloween lineup.

In short, Julie didn't get upset or embarrassed—far from it. And
her assertion that I was the only atheist she'd ever met made me
realize that correcting the general assumption of religious belief
could be a good thing, an important thing, not just for me and my
kids, but for everyone. But in the interactions that followed—with
an aunt at a family event, a teacher at a Christmas concert, or a
high school friend on Facebook—when I mustered the courage to
call myself an atheist, I was often gently invited to recant. "Now
are you an atheist or an agnostic?" they might say. (*Now are you a
lesbian or have you just not met the right boy?*)

Obviously, they wanted to give me, a person who seems nice, a
nicer word. "Atheist" evokes a sneering cynic who thinks believers

(and possibly love and puppies too) are beneath him (yes, him). That's the stereotype. He scoffs at a well-meaning "God bless you." His eye-rolling muscles are the most developed ones in his pale, bookwormy body.

An agnostic, on the other hand, is just a regular person humble enough to admit what she doesn't know. She's not sure there is a God, but she's not sure there isn't. Either way is fine! Believers with even a tiny bit of doubt can relate to the agnostic, which is why they sometimes helpfully offer me that label. They want me to be someone they can understand. They want me to be someone they can like. Maybe they even want me to be someone who can like them.

First, I appreciate the effort. Second, I am tempted. "Agnostic" does suit my personality. I acknowledge the utility of religion, even its virtues, and have no interest in convincing others not to believe. I tend to see all sides of an argument. I am keenly aware of the distance between all I know and all there is to know.

So why don't I call myself an agnostic? Because I see absolutely no reason to think there might be a God. None. I don't see some evidence for and some against. I see no evidence for and plenty against.

To be clear: I really don't think much about whether God exists. I enjoy those British-accented books that sharply articulate every possible argument against God's existence. I'm grateful they did the work, grateful that all that complex reasoning sits on my shelf like an intellectual battery pack. But I don't really need them. My atheism derives naturally from a few simple observations.

1. The Greek myths are obviously stories. The Norse myths are obviously stories. Joseph Smith and L. Ron Hubbard obviously just made that shit up. Extrapolate.

2. Life is confusing and death is scary. Naturally humans want to believe that someone capable is in charge of everything

and that we somehow continue to live after we die. But (2a) wanting doesn't make it so.

3. The holy books that underpin some of the bigger theistic religions are riddled with "facts" now disproved by science and "morality" now disavowed by modern adherents. Extrapolate.

4. The existence of child rape (and other unfathomable cruelties).

As for the argument that God isn't an actual being capable of or interested in preventing (4) but instead is a sort of cosmic life force / sense of oneness / mystical transcendence, well . . . then we're not really talking about theism anymore. If you're not using the term "God" to mean a deity "with the capacity to design, to choose, to create," a being actively engaged in human affairs, and instead using it "as a way of describing Nature itself,"[1] then you're falling into the trap that Daniel Dennett calls "belief in belief in God." He argues in *Breaking the Spell* that we name "a throng of deanthropomorphized, intellectualized concepts" the same thing that believers call their Supreme Being merely so we can say "we all believe in God."[2] That's how ingrained it is in us that we're supposed to believe in "God." We know the God of the Bible doesn't make sense, so we give the title to something else.

We should stop doing that. As long as a large number of people literally believe that God is looking down from heaven, judging our actions, preferring that women wear dresses or what have you, it's just misleading to claim that you believe in God metaphorically. Let's call love "love" and not confuse the issue.

That's it—why I call myself an atheist. It's not some long footnoted debate or tortured intellectual journey. To me, it's clear there is no God. Or rather, it's clear that God is made up: *of course* God exists, as the most powerful, most fascinating, most cited fictional character ever created.

❧

As simple as it is (or could be), being an "atheist" certainly *feels* complicated. Even people who are clear, in their own minds, about the fact that God is made up may avoid calling themselves atheists because it seems like so much work. Your presumed atheistic responsibilities are extremely time-consuming. After you complain to the school board about the daily recitation of the Pledge of Allegiance and sue the town for its pre-meeting prayer policy, you have to picket a Christmas display, debate a Jesuit, carefully re-stamp all the "In God We Trust" mottos on your paper money with "E Pluribus Unum," and try to convince your grandmother not to go to church. It's a full-time job! "Atheist" even sounds like a career: *"What's up with the kids?" "Well, Janie is a nutritionist now, and Abby just got certified as an atheist. She has her own practice down in the city."*

Also, you have to be really, really smart, like PhD-from-Oxford smart, since every self-respecting atheist should be able to explain how the universe came to be and to prove that God doesn't exist. That's your job now. It's not enough just to *read* Richard Dawkins's explanation of why natural selection is the answer to the statistical improbability of the *Euplectella* skeleton, and thus why irreducible complexity fails as an argument for a Creator; you also have to be able to explain it to others. The Big Bang, too, please—explain that.

And you certainly can't like Christmas trees or Bing Crosby or find yourself transfixed and tearful standing in front of Michelangelo's *Pietà*. Atheists are supposed to have no patience or respect for the religious impulse. Don't even think about joining in and enjoying yourself. No more King cake or iftar or matzo ball soup. "God Rest Ye Merry, Gentlemen" must be hereafter put to rest.

Since you don't believe in a Supreme Being that no one has ever proved to be real, you must not believe in *anything* that isn't strictly material or rational. Emotions? Forget it. Forget about being moved by watching a child help another child, by a sunset, by the final measures of Chopin's "Fantaisie-Impromptu." Forget about love.

Anyway, that's the atheist archetype that popular culture has given us, which means that many people who agree with atheism in concept, but who don't feel it as a cause, tend to keep quiet about their beliefs. Needless to say, their reticence adds to the problem. Since many people who don't believe in God hesitate to identify themselves as atheists, the people everyone thinks of as atheists are the hard-core Bible-dumpers. The professionals, the activists, the agitators—not regular people who are busy with things like jobs and kids and cooking. So regular people don't see atheists as regular people—*even if they themselves are atheists.*

But being an atheist doesn't have to be a full-time job or even a hobby. It doesn't have to spring from anger or emerge as misanthropy. Even I, the person writing this book, am capable of going days without thinking about the fact that God is a human invention. I spend more time shopping for clothes on clearance, rearranging leftovers into a passable dinner, and trying to decipher what recent event sparked the newest flurry of knowing tweets.

When I have sex, it's heterosexual. When I sign my name, it's with my left hand. And when I think about the world, there's no God in or above it.

It's that simple. Ask yourself: *Do I think there's a supernatural being in charge of the universe?* If you answer "no," you're an atheist. That's it—you're done. No suing, signing, marching, debating, or tweeting required. You don't have to do anything with that information. But if you do choose to share it, you may find you know far more atheists than you thought.

# WE ARE NOT ALONE

*If you added up all the nominal Christians, Jews, Muslims, Hindus, Buddhists, etc.—those who are religious in name only—who do not take the tenets of the religions very seriously—you really might get the largest denomination in the world.*

GREG EPSTEIN, *Good without God*

HERE'S A TRUE STORY about telling the truth.

Many years ago, a retired doctor—an acquaintance of my mother's—graciously offered to let my son practice on his grand piano while we were vacationing in Virginia. Mom and I brought Jesse over to the good doctor's country estate one Sunday, and, with a Haydn sonata cascading in the background, I was left in the backyard to chat with our host.

I didn't really know the man, but, having grown up in the Shenandoah Valley, I knew the type: kindly exterior, conservative to the core. I thought mournfully of the book I had brought in the hope that our host wouldn't be home, and I resigned myself to making the smallest possible talk for a whole hour. Jesse probably needed two, but one felt like the most I could give.

The doctor and his wife had a hobby business growing and selling flowers, as well as a carefully landscaped home garden. I do not know a lilac from a daylily. So while Dr. Flowers (as I'll call him) showed me around, I struggled to think of questions. Do florists request certain flowers? How fast do the cut ones regrow? How long is the growing season down here?

Yes, I was that boring, and that bored.

We wandered from the greenhouse to a plot of flowers (no, I cannot be more specific) flashing a swirl of burnt orange and maroon: Virginia Tech's school colors, or so I gathered. "I'm a big Hokie fan," Dr. Flowers explained. I'm from Virginia; at least I knew what a Hokie was. But at this point all I could do was nod.

Then we came to a stop at another small patch of not-yet-bloomed blooms surrounding a statue of St. Fiacre (the name helpfully carved on the side), who was the patron saint of gardeners. According to legend, a seventh-century bishop told him he could have as much land for his hermitage as he could surround with a furrow in a day; with God's help, that turned out to be quite a bit.

In a gesture of appreciation, and in the hopes of keeping the conversation off gardening, I offered, "I love saints." (It's true: I do.)

"Now, I know you were raised Jewish," the good doctor replied. "Are you still Jewish?"

This was a turn in the conversation I had not expected and for which I was not prepared.

Whether someone is "still Jewish" is not a question you hear in an area with a sizable Jewish population. Anyone familiar with Jews is also familiar with the concept that being Jewish is as much about belonging as belief. It isn't something you change easily. Or at all. You can be more or less observant, you can downgrade to "culturally" Jewish, but it's hard to give it up entirely. I'm pretty sure you can even convert to Hinduism and still be Jewish.

So Dr. Flowers's question revealed a certain provincialism. But in the tone of his voice, I heard open-mindedness, a willingness to entertain the idea that people change their beliefs. And his question revealed curiosity too. This wealthy, white-haired, round-bellied Southern doctor was truly *curious* about me.

I didn't know how to answer him. Partly because I didn't know the answer—am I still Jewish? Ish?—and partly because I was loath to offend. His sincere question deserved a sincere response, but the word "atheist," as we know, can turn people off.

"Well," I said. "I still like the food! But . . . I don't believe in any supernatural beings." (Still couldn't say it, could I?)

And then Dr. Flowers proceeded to tell me in his silky Southern drawl that he, as a man of science, had a lot of trouble believing the Bible stories—the Easter story, for instance, gave him a lot of pause—and he'd told his pastor so.

He still loved his church, but he bemoaned the way the church often treated people, particularly women and "the gays."

That phrase, "the gays," clanged in my New York ears. Again, my brain struggled to assimilate words that were sort of wrong with a sentiment that was just right.

It turned out that Dr. Flowers's son was gay, and that revelation changed the doctor's mind about a lot of things. "I was bad about it at first, for about a year," he confessed. "I had a really hard time. And then my doctor said to me, did you love your son before you found out he was gay? And I said yes. And he said, is he the same person now as he was then? And, boom! That kind of opened my eyes."

Well, that kind of opened *my* eyes. But it wasn't the only time someone has responded to my honesty with surprising honesty of their own. We all go around—I once did too—assuming that everyone else is a believer. I'll bet every private atheist in America knows someone who thinks they've never met an atheist before. I'll bet every private atheist in America sometimes feels like the only atheist in the room while chatting with another atheist who feels like the only atheist in the room.

We won't know the truth until we tell the truth.

# SORRY, HONEY, GOD'S JUST PRETEND

*If you believe something, you must share it;*
*it's one of the ways we all learn about truth.*

PENN JILLETTE, *God, No!*

A LLOW ME TO INTRODUCE you to my youngest child, my
daughter. You've met my two boys, if only briefly, as little
warm bodies who absorbed my early efforts to explain the world as
I saw it. You'll meet them again soon.

My oldest, Noah, will reveal his natural need to please and the
gift for logic that sometimes conflicts with it. Although Noah could
be relied upon to test the reasonableness of a parent's convictions
about, say, the utility of practicing the piano *years* after he *already*
learned how to play it, he accepted without argument that there
was no God. He was curious only where that left him as a Jew.
More on that later.

His younger brother, Jesse, despite an abiding appreciation for
Grandma's matzo ball soup, had no interest in even pretending
religious belief. He too accepted, as given, the fictional nature of
the Supreme Being, although he gave me a hard time about the
afterlife. He really, really wanted there to be an afterlife. More on
that later.

Then came Lena. She was not worried about death, and she
was not interested in being Jewish. She just wanted to know how
the world worked. She asked everything: how long do chickens
live and what is insurance and how do you remember the way to

all the places you drive and how do *girls* masturbate? Her questions seemed to come from curiosity rather than emotional need.
She wasn't worried or conflicted; her brain was just click-clacking
along, gathering information and building a fully functional scale
model of the world.

One day, in the middle of doing her math homework at age
nine, after having heard a casual remark I made to her father, she
paused, pencil poised, to ask me the obvious but as yet never asked
question: "How do we *know* there's no God?"

It's a question atheists get asked all the time, often by people
who think we should use that gentler term "agnostic," people who
are comfortable with doubt and suspicious of certainty. In answer I
would say that all evidence points to the fact that God is a popular
and useful fiction, and that no evidence points to the fact that he
actually exists.

But how do we know? Where's the evidence that he *doesn't* exist? That's what Lena was asking for. That's what leaves many people wary of leaving the "agnostic" camp, and it's what makes many
parents—even those willing to call themselves atheists—decline
to issue definitive statements to their children. Even people who
accept my atheism with a shrug object to the idea that I teach my
children there is no God. No one taught me to be an atheist, after
all; I came to my own conclusions. Shouldn't my children get the
opportunity to assess the facts and decide for themselves?

The fact that only one of my three children ever challenged me
on this point underscores the great and awesome power of the parent. How can these kids possibly decide for themselves when their
all-powerful mom has decided for them?

It's true I stacked the deck. There's always the chance my children will experience a late-life conversion, but, like smoking, belief in the supernatural is a habit far less likely to be picked up by
adults than by kids. "It would be as difficult to instill into the mind
of a man, forty years old, the extravagant notions that are given
us of the divinity as to eradicate them from the mind of him who

had imbibed them from infancy,"[1] wrote the eighteenth-century French philosopher Paul-Henri Thiry, Baron d'Holbach, in *Good Sense* (which he had the good sense to publish under a pseudonym). I disagree, though: I think it's *more* difficult to learn religious belief later in life than to unlearn it.

So chances were good that teaching my kids there was no God would likely result in . . . their not believing in God. I can't prove that God does not exist. So how can I teach my children as fact something that cannot actually be proven? Isn't that intellectually irresponsible?

Well, I can't prove that monsters don't exist, either, but I have no trouble saying to my kids, "Monsters are pretend." What, after all, is the alternative?

"Mommy, are monsters real?"

"Well, honey, I don't believe monsters are real and neither does your father. Certainly, we've never seen one. But a lot of people do believe they are real. What do you think?"

Of course not. Monsters are pretend. No one would accuse me of indoctrinating my children with a nonbelief in monsters or of brainwashing them with my skepticism about the paranormal. And yet that's precisely what happens when the subject is God.

So what's the difference? One friend has suggested that because monsters are scary, it's okay to act certain about them. Leaving the monster question unresolved doesn't do anyone any good and might result in some sleepless nights for all concerned. On the other hand, children might think it's nice to believe in heaven or God or fairies, so parents should leave open those more pleasant possibilities.

She has a point. Belief in God *seems* harmless enough. What's the harm in imagining that a kindly old man runs the world? There is none—as long as they know it's not actually true. Being able to tell fact from fiction comes in quite handy in life, personally and politically, and at least one study[2] has shown that kids who are raised with religion can't do that as well as kids who are raised without it. So, sure, let's imagine Great-Grandma looking down at us from heaven, but let's be clear we are *making that up*. And because our surrounding culture tells us, over and over, that heaven *might* be true, we have to be extra clear that the heaven scenario is no more plausible than the idea that Great-Grandma's spirit has been distilled in a bottle of scotch. When the kids are old enough, they can have a sip. Or that Great-Grandma now haunts the 793s of the public library; where, in the Dewey decimal system would they like to be filed?

Let's leave the poor dead lady alone for a minute as we pause to imagine that world events are directed by the seemingly random path a ladybug takes down our sidewalk. Or to think that we could be, as my son Jesse once posited, characters in someone else's dream.

It's okay—not just okay: mind-expanding, pleasurable—to think about these things. To picture an alternate universe and ponder its metaphorical significance. I'm happy to do that and happy for my kids to. But I would never say such speculative flights of fancy are or even might be factually true, and I would never say that of heaven or God, either. Just as I would never say, "It could be that a ladybug is in charge; one day you can decide for yourself," I would never say, "*I* don't think God is in charge, but who knows?"

I taught my children there is no God. Or, to be more accurate, I taught them that there are lots and lots of gods, all of them fascinating and all of them invented by human beings. What I'm supposed to do, according to many guides on nonreligious parenting, is different: be honest with them about what their dad and I believe but present as equally valid what other people believe. Give them all the options. Jane Wynne Willson, in *Parenting Without God: Experiences of a Humanist Mother*, offers this imagined conversation as a guide:

"Miss Higginson says that Mandy has gone to Heaven to be with Jesus."

"Yes, I know that Miss Higginson thinks that, and of course Grandma believes in Heaven too. But Dad and I think rather differently . . . When you're a bit older you can make up your own mind."[3]

Wendy Thomas Russell in *Relax, It's Just God*, proposes this answer to a child's question, "Is God real?"

No one knows for sure, but many people think so. Even though they can't see God, they believe in him, and that is called faith. Not everyone has faith, but lots of people do. It's okay to believe in God, and it's okay not to believe in God.[4]

Deborah Mitchell, in *Growing Up Godless: A Parent's Guide to Raising Kids without Religion*, says she was worried at first about biasing her children toward her views of religion, but she reassures herself and the reader that it's okay, since she was just one source of information among many:

For critics who worry that I've tainted my kids . . . I'm sure I have, but they've also been tainted . . . by their friends and family members who believe, too. So I guess it all evens out in the end because they are equally influenced by believers and nonbelievers. At some point, I figure they will have the emotional maturity and the information they need to decide for themselves what they do or do not believe.[5]

Some people take their children to a round robin of area churches and synagogues so they can make an informed choice. Giving them all the options sounds nice and progressive and open-minded. But do all the options include the option to believe that the Earth is only six thousand years old? Or that homosexuality is immoral? Or that women are subservient to men?

Each of those beliefs is something they could learn among the local religious offerings. Not just fiction posing as fact, but also, in some cases, wrong posing as right. Shall I refrain from imposing my moral values on my children as well?

Let's consider a few more imaginary conversations:

> "Teddy says wives have to do whatever their husbands say. Is that true?"

> "You know, people disagree about that. I think women and men are equal, but a lot of people don't. It sure is an interesting question!"

> *or*

> "My teacher says it's now legal for men to marry other men. That's gross, isn't it?"

> "No, I don't think it's gross. I think two adults who love each other should be able to get married. But some people think marriage should only be between a man and a woman. They think men who want to marry other men are doomed to burn in hell for all eternity. When you get older, you can decide for yourself."

Not a chance.

I could take my kids to visit only the houses of worship whose values accord with mine: the extra-Reform Jews, the Unitarians, or progressive Episcopalians. But if I did that, I would still be limiting their options and pushing them to believe certain things rather than others. To what extent, precisely, do I let my children make up their own minds about life? What lessons do I teach and what do I refrain from teaching, lest I influence them too much?

Dale McGowan, editor of *Parenting beyond Belief*, says he follows every statement of worldview with something like, "But that's just my opinion. You have to figure out your opinion." Strictly speaking, that's true: they *will* figure out their own opinions. And, sure, they might end up rejecting a few that their mother presented as obviously and inarguably correct. Maybe at some point they'll decide that, in fact, there is such a thing as too much butter. In the meantime, as a parent, I am not willing to say "that's just my opinion" about whether something is fact or fiction, right or wrong. All beliefs—mine, theirs, Mike Pence's—are not equal. Many are wrong. Some are harmlessly wrong (I'll go to heaven after I die), and some are harmfully wrong (gay people will go to hell after they die).

So although my children were free to question me, although I didn't mock them when they broached the subject of God's existence, although I didn't forbid them to speak of an afterlife, I refused to step back. I engaged them, drew out their ideas, contemplated and contended with their points. Did I exploit "the parent-offspring link" that is the "major pathway of transmission of religion,"[6] as Daniel Dennett describes it? Yes. Did I have an unfair advantage because I was older and I knew how to argue and they had to come to me for food? Yes, and I used that advantage as much as I could before I lost it. To the best of my ability—and against the prevailing winds of my culture—I set out to raise feminists who acknowledge that society has a fundamental responsibility to the weakest among us, who prefer scratch food to anything that comes in a box, and who have an accurate picture of their place in the universe.

*How do we know, Lena? We know the way we know there are no fairies: the only proof is man-made and all the thinking behind it is wishful. We know because we are open to evidence and we have been given none. We know because—*

But she had gone back to her fractions.

# HUBRIS

*Nothing seems crazy when you're used to it.*
SARAH SILVERMAN, *We Are Miracles*

"MONSTERS ARE JUST PRETEND" is different from "God is just pretend" because monsters are scary (as my friend argued), but also—and this is even more important—because *most grownups don't believe in monsters.* Teaching your children that something imaginary doesn't exist is perfectly fine; teaching them that something imaginary doesn't exist when most people think it does is—to many—suspect, transgressive, and possibly even abusive.

Vampires, zombies, woodland sprites, the denizens of Mount Olympus, and the Christian God are *all* pretend: magical, invisible beings whose existence cannot be disproved. Logically, fairies, Ares, and Jehovah all fall into the same category: fictional characters. But culturally? Not even close.

As I write, assorted polls find that at least 81 percent of Americans believe in God,[1] 40 percent believe God created the Earth during the past ten thousand years,[2] and three-quarters believe in heaven.[3] Our calendar year is counted from the supposed birth of a deity (and the months and days of the week are named for other, passé deities); our work weeks pause for the sabbath; our school vacations conveniently leave room for Christmas and Easter; our money states "In God We Trust"; witnesses in jury trials swear on Bibles that they will tell the truth "so help me God"; and so many political speeches end with "God Bless America" that you would think it was just the official way to say "this speech is over."

In this context, it's hard—even for me—to remember that religion is all made up. It's relatively easy with new religions, like Scientology (with its Galactic Confederacy and its meat bodies) or even the Church of Latter Day Saints. (Okay, so after Joseph Smith translated the golden plates buried outside his house by looking at seer stones in the bottom of his hat, he gave them back to the Angel Moroni and *that's why* we can't look at them now?) But mainstream Christianity, Judaism, and Islam—the time-honored, people's-choice myths—are so familiar and so broadly accepted that they feel true-ish, and shrugging them off or laughing at them or flatly denying their validity feels arrogant. So many people believe—who am I not to? So many people believe—shouldn't I give belief at least the benefit of my children's doubt? So many people believe—isn't it an act of hubris to teach my children those people have it wrong?

Yes. It is.

We use "hubris" to mean excessive arrogance and pride, but it has a more specific religious meaning: it's pride that leads one to challenge the gods. One foundational Greek myth that expresses this concept is the story of Icarus, who used wings his father made to escape the Minotaur's Labyrinth but ignored his father's warnings not to fly too high, lest the sun melt the wax that held his wings together. I had always thought it was Icarus who displayed hubris in this story—he's the one who overshoots his prescribed limits and suffers the consequences—but when I reread Ovid, I realized it's Daedalus, the father, who ventures first above his station, building an invention that "altered the natural order of things."[4]

We're not supposed to challenge the order of things or question—or worse, try to change—our place in the universe. A less famous, more horrific story of hubris involves Niobe, Queen of Thebes. In the midst of a celebration at the altar of the goddess Latona (Leto for the Greeks), Niobe declares (according to

Ovid) that they should worship her, Niobe, instead. After all, she's wealthy, beautiful, and powerful too. "What madness, to prefer the gods you are told about to the ones you see?"[5] Besides, she has seven sons and seven daughters, while Latona has only one of each, namely Artemis and Apollo.

Ovid mercilessly ramps up the dramatic irony in the speech that follows:

> I am fortunate (indeed, who can deny it?) and I will stay fortu-
> nate (and who can doubt that too?). My riches make me safe. I
> am greater than any whom Fortune can harm, and though she
> could take much away, she would leave me much more. Surely
> my comforts banish fear. Imagine that some of this host of
> children could be taken from me, I would still not, bereaved,
> be reduced to the two of Latona's family.[6]

I think we can all see where this is going. Apollo proceeds to kill all of Niobe's sons, one by one, in gory fashion, after which Niobe's husband kills himself. And still Niobe manages to taunt Latona—"After so many deaths, I still outdo you!"—and then Artemis kills the daughters, one by one, down to the last. "Leave me just one, the youngest! I only ask for one, the youngest of all!" begs Niobe.

Despite Ovid's oversell of Niobe's hubris (which in other sources comes down to a single maternal boast), despite her stupidity (which is not always a feature of rebellious mortals—Arachne wasn't stupid), and despite the cartoonish nature of the violence ("The rush of blood . . . spurted high in the air, in a long jet"), Niobe's plea—"Leave me just one, the youngest!"—still makes me cry. As does the subsequent predictable death related with devastating understatement: "While she prayed, she, for whom she prayed, was dead."

What brings Niobe to this horrifying end? Her denial of the divine. The gods are no better than she, she claims, and besides, you can't even see them. She even stops other people from worshipping: "Go home—enough of holy things—and take those laurel wreaths from your hair!" The Greeks had a word for pitting mortal power against the gods, denying their potency and therefore, on some level, their divinity: "theomachy." Historian and classicist Tim Whitmarsh explains, in *Battling the Gods*, that theomachy wasn't sinful—the Greeks didn't have sin—it was just dumb: "a horrible misjudgment of the odds."[7]

Future religions, however, saw the rejection of gods as a threat rather than a personal error and brutally punished the flock when it strayed. The Old Testament God killed the Israelites who, after growing tired of waiting for Moses to descend from Mount Sinai, made a golden calf they proceeded to worship. The most carefully spelled out of the Ten Commandments prohibits this same crime— the crime of disloyalty to God—and promises vengeance not just on those who commit it but also on their children "to the third and fourth generation of those who reject me" (Deuteronomy 5:9).

In Islam, too, pride and unbelief go together. After he creates the world, God tells the angels to worship Adam, and they do, except for Iblīs: "He refused and waxed arrogant, and was among the unbelievers" (Quran 2:34).[8] He is promptly cast out of heaven, just like Lucifer, the Judeo-Christian God's top angel, who decides to challenge God's supremacy—he wants to place his throne "above the stars of God" (Isaiah 14:13). As the embodiment of hubris, the greatest of all sins, Lucifer comes to represent evil itself.

Of Catholicism's Seven Deadly Sins (lust, greed, gluttony, sloth, wrath, envy, and pride), pride is supposed to be the first, the worst, the root of all the others. In a chapter entitled "The Great Sin" in *Mere Christianity*, C. S. Lewis calls pride "the complete anti-God state of mind."[9] *The Catholic Encyclopedia* calls pride "a species of contempt of God."[10] It is the opposite of submission—a rejection of one's assigned place in the metaphysical hierarchy. It's a refusal to subject oneself to divine authority, a step toward rejecting God altogether.

So, yes, telling my children that God is made up is the *defi-nition* of hubris. Telling my children that there is no heaven is exactly the sort of thing the Greek gods would punish by turn-ing me into a spider or a rock. And it is exactly the sort of thing that would get me barred from paradise, whether I be Muslim or Catholic.

Fortunately, for me and for my children, all that stuff is made up. I don't have to worry about hell any more than I have to worry about Apollo shooting avenging arrows into the narrow chests of my young boys.

·◌·

But my hubris does cost something. Atheism doesn't just mean not believing in God; it means not *having* a god. Even though God is a made-up character, he's got a lot to offer believers. Consolation in the face of death—that's a big one. A ready-made framework for moral decision-making. Holidays, which are more important than they would seem. Words to channel joy and gratitude, wonder and angst. Ceremonies to mark life changes. Relief from bearing ulti-mate responsibility for the world.

It would be fair to argue that all those things, except for the final one, really come from religion, not God, per se. I could have kept the religion without believing in the supernatural being at its core, without believing its dogma is literally true. Lots of people do this—and lots of people *have been doing this* for thousands of years. "It might in fact be perfectly rational to honor the gods pub-licly without believing that they exist," wrote Sextus Empiricus in the second century.[11] People at all ends of the Truth Spectrum use religion as the framework for their lives.

Oh, you haven't heard of the Truth Spectrum? It's my (com-pletely made up) way of categorizing religious attitudes, and it has nothing to do with whether your scriptures are true. It just mea-sures how true *you believe them* to be. From most to least:

**"Literally true."** You believe your Holy Text to be factual. To put this in terms of, say, Passover, that means you believe God actually appeared to Moses "in a flame of fire out of a bush" (Exodus 3:2).

**"Mostly true."** You believe your Holy Text to be generally true, but sometimes figurative or evocative rather than literal. Did the Red Sea literally part so the Israelites could walk on dry ground, "the waters forming a wall for them on their right and on their left" (Exodus 14:22)? Okay, maybe not. But the parting of the Red Sea represents the power of God, and it was truly the power of God that permitted the Israelites to escape from Egypt, against seemingly insurmountable odds.

**"There is truth in this."** You believe that your Holy Text contains some historical, scientific, and even ethical errors. But you can overlook these errors and focus on the wisdom to be found there: the psychological insights, for instance, that explain how the oppressed sometimes shrink from their own deliverance "because of their broken spirit and their cruel slavery" (Exodus 6:9) and how great leaders are sometimes reluctant leaders: "O my Lord, please send someone else," says Moses (Exodus 4:13).

**"I can use this to make truth."** You believe that the text in question is fictional but still useful. This attitude is cousin to what Tim Whitmarsh describes, in *Battling the Gods*, as the "deeply rooted Greek idea that myth, however mythical, contains a grain of truth."[12] The Burning Bush, the Ten Plagues, and the Parting of the Red Sea either didn't happen or have been profoundly altered in the retelling. But the resonant imagery and dialogue, the traditional songs, and the annual injunction to tell the Exodus story give you an opportunity to talk with your kids about oppression, liberation movements, and human rights.

**"Bullshit."** You believe you should teach your kids about oppression, liberation movements, and human rights by talking about . . . oppression, liberation movements, and human rights. No need to look at the issues through a murky lens of ancient, patriarchal, sectarian stories. Why use things you don't believe in to talk about things you *do* believe in? Why start with processed foods when you can start from scratch?

That's it. That's the Truth Spectrum™: from simply true to simply not.

Even in a society whose religious beliefs appear to be monolithic, any individual might fall anywhere on this spectrum. Maybe most Greeks at some point thought Zeus truly turned himself into a swan. But even then, I'm sure there were people crying, "Bullshit! Leda made that up." All the way back in the twelfth century, the Jewish philosopher Maimonides said of Genesis, "The account given in scripture is not, as is generally believed, intended to be in all its parts literal."[13] In other words, "Mostly true."

Also, people and religions can change over time, and therefore move from one point on the spectrum to another. In *The Atheist Muslim*, Ali Rizvi writes that "the more progress humanity has made over time in everything from medical science to civil rights, the more 'metaphorical' scripture has become."[14] As a young man, he attempted to square the Quran's magical verses with reality and its violent verses with morality. "I used every interpretive tool I could dig up, and I got very good at it."[15] His friends and family were good at it too. How did they interpret Muhammed's journey to heaven on a winged horse, for instance? "The explanation was that Muhammed flew at the speed of light, in the form of energy," writes Rizvi. "The horse, of course, was a metaphor."[16]

Or at least that's how his cohort of modern, progressive Muslims saw it. Religious authorities themselves also sometimes choose metaphor over literal truth. Sister Wendy Beckett, in her book on prayer, writes that the Catholic Church will eventually change its attitude toward sexuality. As it is now, she says, "Some strictures of the Old Testament are still taken literally, whereas others—like the profaning proximity of a menstruating woman—are not."[17] When the Church evolves, it will do so (as it has before) by moving its interpretation of the scriptures further down the Truth Spectrum from literal fact toward instructive allegory and metaphor.

This move from literal to figurative, by the way, is precisely the journey Santa Claus takes when a child learns the truth, transforming seamlessly from an actual man who flies around delivering presents to a fictional character and embodiment of the spirit of Christmas. (The reindeer, my dear, is a metaphor.)

You might think I would stand smack in the "Bullshit" camp. Most days I do. But I majored in comparative literature, which means that I learned how to make truth from *anything*. I could have continued along that path. I could have used my word-loving, idea-grappling brain to turn every Bible story into an allegory, every prayer into a metaphor, every holiday into a teachable moment, and every reference to heaven or the afterlife into speculative musings. Honestly, I'd enjoy that. It would be a fantastic puzzle, like trying to make dinner out of whatever you can buy in a convenience store.

Why try to make sense of life from scratch when you can just gussy up a precooked religious tradition that's been kept warm under a heat lamp?

Well, to extend this metaphor a little more: because it tastes better. Because I know what's in it. Because it's better for me, and better for all of us. And because in learning how to cook up, say, morality, for myself, I develop an understanding of what it's made of, I appreciate it more, and I come away fuller, with the satisfaction not just of having consumed but of having created.

There's also the satisfaction that comes from telling the truth. Sometimes I think atheists have something in common with sincerely religious people: we are drawn to authenticity. We think that what we say and do about the world matters and that pretending, passing, going through the motions, and putting off hard questions until later are all ways of not living fully. They are all a betrayal of ourselves, a waste of our short time on earth. In *For Small Creatures Such as We*, Sasha Sagan writes about how, when her grandfather told *his* father, an Orthodox Jew, that he didn't believe in God, the elder replied, "The only sin would be to pretend."[18]

I understand why people pretend, why they stick with the religion of their childhoods, even if pretending makes them a little uncomfortable. "There are countless reasons why people are part of a religion other than—and sometimes even *in spite of*—the supernatural elements," writes Phil Zuckerman in *Society without God*.[19] Wanting to please people, get along with others, avoid offense or hubris—all of that. Being reluctant to contradict what everyone in the world seems to believe is true. That too.

But there's more. Often they think religion is the only way to get—and to give their children—the things they need or want in life, including answers to our most urgent and confusing questions: How do we console ourselves in the face of our mortality? Should we make new holidays when the old ones don't fit? How do we learn right from wrong? Do we even need whatever it is people find in a house of worship? Can atheists pray—or is that crazy? What do we do about rites of passage that originate in a faith we don't believe in? And what do we get when we give up the notion of a higher power?

"Why do people want religion at all?" ask sociologists Rodney Stark and Roger Finke in *Acts of Faith*.[20] "They want it because religion is the only plausible source of certain rewards for which there is an inexhaustible demand."

But I am here to tell you that it's not. Religion is not the only source—not even close.

# Part Two

# WHAT WE LOSE AND WHAT WE GAIN

⌀

*The real issue is not whether God exists or not, but where to take the argument once one decides that he evidently doesn't.*

ALAIN DE BOTTON, *Religion for Atheists*

# LIFE WITH NO AFTER

*Soon I will be done with the troubles of the world,*
*Goin' home to live with God.*
*I want to meet my mother,*
*I want to meet my mother,*
*I want to meet my mother.*
*Goin' home to live with God.*

"Soon I Will Be Done," trad.

WHEN MY DAUGHTER WAS three years old, my friend's three-year-old daughter died. I heard about this tragedy secondhand. My friend and I had been close when I was a teenager, but by the time we had children, we had grown apart. When my parents called to let me know, I tried to imagine what my friend and his wife went through that day—the worry, the hope, the panic, the devastating realization that their baby was gone—and then right away I tried not to.

Instead, I reminded myself that they were born-again Christians. They believed, as they wrote then, that their daughter had gone to heaven, that God had called her to be with him, that she was now dancing with Jesus, and that one day, after their deaths, they would see her again. I was grateful for that. I was grateful that they could comfort themselves with the thought that she was just somewhere else, somewhere infinitely better. They felt pain, but she didn't; they were sad, but she was happy in the arms of God. I would never want to take that belief away from them.

I could never have it myself, though. I can't make myself believe. And yet when I think about death, I understand why people want to.

Science has solved many of the mysteries that religion once sought to clear up. We no longer need Persephone's marriage problems to account for the seasons; we no longer look to He-lios's daily chariot rides to explain the apparent movement of the sun. We now understand the natural (rather than supernat-ural) phenomena that caused floods and plagues and even the occasional parting (and reddening) of a sea. Most people today either disregard or interpret metaphorically the parts of their mythology that science has rendered moot. But they continue to take as gospel the religious explanation for the one human experience people still don't comprehend: what happens to you after you die.

Death—shocking, predictable, universal, life-shaping, "the most important fact about us,"[1] according to philosopher Todd May—is what we humans struggle most to explain to ourselves. It may well be the reason religion exists. Anthropologist Pascal Boy-er, in *Religion Explained*, writes, "Mortality, it would seem, naturally produces *questions* that religion answers and *emotions* that it helps alleviate."[2] In *A Short History of Myth*, Karen Armstrong writes that myth "is nearly always rooted in the experience of death and the fear of extinction," a "counternarrative" created by early peoples to help them come to terms with their mortality.[3]

Lewis Black writes, in *Me of Little Faith*, "Death is the abiding mystery."[4]

But is it really a mystery? The fact that we die may feel horribly unfair, but what happens after we die is fairly obvious to the na-ked eye, no advanced scientific thought required. If early humans didn't understand it, it wasn't for lack of carbon dating or statistical modeling. They didn't understand it because they didn't *want* to.

HUMAN 1 [musing over lifeless corpse]
If only we knew what happened when a person died.

HUMAN 2 [burying a dead animal]
I know, man. It's just a *complete mystery*.

HUMAN 3 [holding a skull]
Do you think maybe we're just over, done, nothing, and we turn into objects again instead of people?

HUMAN 1 [scattering someone's ashes]
What? No, don't be dumb. It's got something to do with St. Peter.

Death is a mystery only because we insist that it is. Otherwise, we'd have to accept the observable fact, as yet unrefuted by any evidence, that when people die, they disappear—instantly, in terms of their being, and, in terms of their bodies, after a period of decomposition. They simply cease to exist.

Oops, sorry, did I say "they"? I meant "we"—*we* cease to exist. Keeping our future nonexistence in our heads is such a cognitive challenge that our brains usually spare us the trouble. In Tolstoy's *The Death of Ivan Ilych*, a colleague who comes to pay his respects after Ivan's death is briefly terrified that he too might die, but then somehow—"he did not himself know how"—he snapped out of it and reassured himself that "it should not and could not happen to him." He then goes on to ask about the details of his friend's final days "as though death was an accident natural to Ivan Ilych but certainly not to himself."[5]

When the narrative shifts to show us Ilych's entire life, we learn that Ilych himself, *while dying*, is similarly in denial:

> In the depth of his heart he knew he was dying, but not only was he not accustomed to the thought, he simply did not and could not grasp it. The syllogism he had learnt from Kiesewetter's Logic: "Caius is a man, men are mortal, therefore Caius is mortal," had always seemed to him correct as applied to Caius, but certainly not as applied to himself.[6]

How could I just vanish into nothing? I do not and cannot grasp it.

If I were religious, I wouldn't have to. I might be afraid of the pain of dying, and I might mourn my missing loved ones, but I could rest assured that we would continue to exist even after our bodies had sustained, as per the Uniform Determination of Death Act, "irreversible cessation of circulatory and respiratory functions, or irreversible cessation of all functions of the entire brain."[7] Irreversible, but not, if you're a believer, insurmountable. Simply put, as May writes in *Death*, "In having an afterlife, you survive your own death."[8] Maybe that means you're reincarnated (if you're Hindu), or maybe it means you await a messianic future (if you're Jewish), or maybe it means you're dancing with Jesus in heaven (if you're Christian). From the Bible and the Quran, respectively:

> Jesus said to her, "I am the resurrection and the life. Those who believe in me, even though they die, will live, and everyone who lives and believes in me will never die." (John 11:25–26)

> O thou soul at peace! Return unto thy Lord, content, contenting. Enter among My servants. Enter my garden. (Quran 89:27–30)

May points out that these aren't vague we-all-return-to-the-soup-of-human-consciousness assurances. These are promises that *you personally* will continue to exist. "The thing that death threatens to take away"—the self—"will remain more or less intact,"[9] he writes. It wouldn't make sense to move up the karmic ladder (as Hindus believe) if you just turned into a completely different soul every time you returned to earth; your *particular* soul has to make the journey. And the fact that you will remain *you* in the afterlife is the nearly irresistible signing bonus of Christianity. You will hold your loved ones in your arms again. Thus St. Paul taunts in 1 Corinthians 15:55, "Where, O death, is your victory? / Where, O death, is your sting?"

It's a neat solution, sidestepping the dead body, so to speak, and insisting that the part of you that lives on is *the invisible part*.

Given this promise, you would think that believers would not fear death or even do much to avoid it. You would assume they would celebrate their own or their loved ones' impending deaths, looking forward as they do to "a life of joy and peace." But do they? In *The Atheist Muslim*, Ali Rizvi recounts his cousin's death from cancer, at age three, when Rizvi was five. He was told she was in heaven, "the best place in the universe," and he remembers thinking, "Why, then, don't we all go there right now? Why are we still here? Why are we so sad for her? Shouldn't we be happy?"[10] May posits that believers still have doubts about the end (or rather the new beginning) they've been promised. He writes, "Belief can push against death, but doubt allows death to push back."[11] I think it's possible to believe in an afterlife but not really *feel* the truth of it, immersed as one is in the realities of living and the desire to go on living. Still, whether or not they always use it, believers do possess a conceptual shield against their own mortality and a fire to warm them in the brutal cold of mourning. As Presbyterian minister Timothy Keller writes, "Any Christian man or woman has the power to triumph over death."[12]

Atheists do not have that power, Keller points out. "Religion gave people tools to help in facing our most formidable foe, and modern secularism has not come up with anything to compensate for its loss."[13] It's a strangely pragmatic way for a pastor to put it—from his perspective, isn't heaven a truth rather than a tool?—but it's a fair point. How *do* atheists face humanity's most formidable foe?

First, I suppose, we can look away. After all, the foe is going to win eventually; in the meantime, our best way to "win" is not to be afraid, not to spend any of our limited time worrying about our time limit. Not thinking about death is a popular strategy among the pragmatists of the world. In *Hamlet*'s graveyard scene, Hamlet, obsessed with mortality, asks Horatio if one couldn't imagine the "noble dust" of even Alexander the Great himself eventually plugging a hole in a barrel. Horatio says dryly, "'Twere to consider too curiously, to consider so."[14] In other words, let's not. Hamlet does not take this advice. But if you're lucky, and you're not being taunted by your dead father's ghost, you can avoid considering too curiously for quite some time. Ivan Ilych manages to avoid it well into his illness and then, once he can't, he wishes he could. He looks back wistfully at the "current of thoughts" that "had formerly shut off, hidden, and destroyed his consciousness of death."[15] Don't want to think about death? Ride that current of thoughts; let it carry you along from day to day, distracting you from the inevitable approach of your final day.

Humans are good at this, until we're not. Hamlet can't avoid thoughts of death from the moment he sees his father's ghost and has to decide whether to kill himself or his uncle or both. Ivan Ilych can—until the final stages of a painful disease. But even if we remain unhaunted and unafflicted, even if we are as sensible and pragmatic as Horatio, even if we develop a perfect system for ignoring the inevitable, death ultimately finds a way to insist on our attention. Airplanes falter. Pandemics encroach. Loved ones die.

·◇·

For most of my life, I took Horatio's advice: I did not consider death too curiously. At the funerals of my grandparents, I managed to adopt the attitude sympathetically lampooned by Tolstoy: essentially, death is something that happens to grandparents, but *certainly not* to me. My own near misses on the highway spiked my adrenaline but did not simultaneously convince me of my mortality. It was not until I had to explain death to my children that I began to think about how to explain it to myself.

The first death in my children's lives was the death of a dog. When Noah was two years old, his uncle's German shepherd died. When we heard the news, we worried about what to say to Noah, whose tiny, happy world included that dog. I knew enough not to say that the dog was "put to sleep," lest Noah associate going to bed with disappearing altogether, and I knew I couldn't say "gone away," either. A mythical farm was no better than a mythical heaven. I refused to lie. But the word "died" would be meaningless to him; I would have to introduce the bizarre idea that a dog could just stop *being* one day. This idea was connected in my mind to other, far scarier ideas: my death, his death, accidental deaths, murder. When I think the word "death," everything I know about the terrible finiteness of human life crowds my brain.

But that was my mind, not his. Noah's brain didn't have any of that information in it yet. That was the problem—I'd have to start from scratch—but it was also the key. The fact that the word "dead" was meaningless to Noah meant that I could use it without setting off a chain reaction. Attaching the accurate, truthful word "dead" to a dog's permanent absence and a man's temporary grief would be the beginning of Noah's understanding of the word. Like "love," an abstract concept we refer to without thinking we have to explain it, "death" would gather weight and meaning for him as he went through life.

And so it did. Through books and movies and his limited life experience (the family cat, his brother's fish), death gradually entered his consciousness and his understanding with hardly any help from me. He accepted the concept but did not appear to worry about it. One night when he was eight, I went to kiss him goodnight and turn off his reading light, and I found him quietly crying over the death of Dumbledore. As a writer, I was thrilled that marks on a page could conjure a world so real that it could move him to tears. But as a mom I was relieved that he'd then fallen asleep easily and awakened happy again. He felt only passing sadness, not prolonged despair.

His brother, Jesse, was different. For him, death was a chasm filled with sorrow; he was drawn to it but afraid to get too close. As a child, he avoided depictions not just of violence, but of tragedy. When he was six, he loved Grieg's *Peer Gynt* suites, which his grandmother had played for him, and he begged to hear the music over and over—most of it, that is. Op. 46, part 2, "Ase's Death," was, for him, unbearably sad. We had to skip that part. From the backseat of the car, he pointed out cemeteries when we drove past—cemeteries in my own town that I had never noticed. When he learned a new song, he would check to see if there was sorrow in its provenance: "Is Stevie Wonder dead?" he would ask, worried. He obsessed about who would die when and how old he would be. And he would push, push, push me on the question of the afterlife.

"We don't actually know *what* happens after you die, right?" he said one night, when I was tucking him in. Blond hair, green eyes, bottom bunk. "I mean, you can't talk to someone who's dead, after all. There *could* be a heaven."

"Well, that's true," I replied, granting him the logic, stalling. I wasn't ready to point out that we *did* know what happens, as much as we can know anything. But I didn't want to promise something untrue. I thought for a moment as I knelt and stroked his arm. Orangutan poster, pale-blue carpet, past bedtime. "But here's the thing: we could sit here right now and make up some other cool thing that could happen when you die, like your soul turns into liquid that evaporates and condenses into rain, so all you know now is sprinkled over the earth when you're gone. *And that's just as likely to be true as heaven is.*" In other words, heaven was made up. Even in the face of his fears, I refused to promise him an afterlife.

## SUSAN WOULD NEVER DO THAT

How could I not do the easiest thing in the world: use the promise of heaven to help my child get to sleep? What kind of a monster was I? Much, much later, I read Sasha Sagan's *For Small Creatures Such as We* and recognized myself in a story she told about her father. As a child worried about death, she would call out to her parents before bed, "'Don't forget! Don't die!' and every evening," she writes, "my mother would say, 'I promise,' and my dad, accuracy zealot that he was, would say, 'I'll do my best.'"[16] So I'm not the only one! But I venture few parents would have been such sticklers for the truth. In fact, I knew people who used religion deliberately for its anti-anxiety properties, accuracy be damned.

One day I was dropping off my daughter for a sleepover at her friend Grace's house, and I paused in the doorway to confirm the pick-up time with Grace's mom, Susan. She said I'd need to fetch Lena in time for her daughter to get to Mass the next day. Something about the tone of Susan's voice when she talked about church made me keep asking questions. She did not hesitate to tell me: No, indeed, she did not like the place. Attending Mass was something she endured only so that her child could receive first communion, and she had to receive first communion if she ever wanted to marry in the church. "But there must be something you get out of it?" I pressed. "Well," she said, "Grace is a very fearful kid, so it's nice to give her something to believe in. When she worries about death and stuff." "In that case," I said, emboldened, "keep her away from *my* daughter—she knows when we're gone, we're gone." We laughed and I left, marveling as I drove that a churchgoing Catholic would be so honest with herself and with me. She was using heaven and God like a security blanket and a pacifier, and she wasn't pretending they were anything else. Except to her child, of course.

My daughter was friends with Susan's daughter, but the real reason Lena loved sleeping over there was Susan. I did not take personally her affection for another mother. I myself grew up in an old farmhouse with books and a bar and what I now understand was grad-school furniture, a house where we kids were more likely to be permitted a glass of chianti than a Coke. When I visited my friends in their suburban homes, I would luxuriate in the feeling of being in a "real house," with wall-to-wall carpeting, matching furniture, and plural TVs. I think that's how Lena felt about Susan: she was a "real mom," with a makeup drawer and single-serving snacks and what seemed like endless patience for the children in her care.

Using heaven and God to create a safe mental and emotional space for their children was what Real Moms did. That was the norm—the ideal even—that I spurned the moment I said, "Sorry, honey," and took heaven away from my worried son. Just for the record, I also love my children, and I also wanted to protect them from fear. Indeed, keeping my kids from being afraid was one of my top concerns. When I lost them for a moment in the library or in a grocery store, I would (quietly) freak out until I found them, not because I was worried about actual harm—getting kidnapped, say, or stuck in the freezer case—but because I was worried about *felt* harm. Fear, anxiety, panic. The same went for death. Yes, I did my best to keep them alive—they wore their seatbelts and their helmets, they got their vaccines and ate their vegetables—but I also wanted them not to live in fear of death. But how do you keep children from fearing death without recourse to a beautiful story about how, even when your body is finished, your *self* never ends?

How do you soothe their fears without heaven?

Well, how do *I* do it for myself?

First I try to put aside my worry that my children will miss me and my angst about all the things I have so far failed to do, and leave myself with just the idea of my own vanishing. If I can manage to do that, death isn't actually that scary. I will be, utterly and completely, gone. All my worries and concerns are someone else's now—unless they were unfounded, in which case they died with me. My work is done—unfinished, half finished, total crap—what do I care? On the other side of whatever physical or psychological pain there is in dying is . . . nothing. Looking at death from the perspective of the dead can be immensely reassuring.

"Death is nothing to us," wrote the Greek philosopher Epicurus sometime around 300 BCE, "since every good and evil lie in sensation. However, death is the deprivation of sensation."[17] It's a supremely simple but effective thought. You could look at the dead

LIFE WITH NO AFTER

bird at your feet and remember that you're going to be dead one day and separated from all that you love. Or you could look at the tiny lifeless body and realize that the bird—or what was once a bird, the afterbird—clearly doesn't mind.

> While we exist, death is not present, and whenever death is present, we do not exist. It is nothing either to the living or the dead, since it does not exist for the living, and the dead no longer are.[18]

I find this thought enormously comforting. Yet the philosopher Kieran Setiya, arguing against Epicurus, writes that "the misfortune of being dead is the misfortune of an absence, a lack, a void of whatever it is that makes life worth living."[19] "No more art, no more knowledge, no more time with friends, nothing."[20] That does sound awful. But who will experience this "drab, insipid future"? Not me! *I won't be there.* Anything I can imagine that involves sensation (darkness, cold, floating, longing) will be wrong. I can stop thinking about how death will feel, because it won't. (But I can reassure myself that it will not feel bad. Not in the slightest.)

I wish I could tell you that, after I came to this conclusion, I never again worried about dying. I can't. But I can say that when I need to calm my fears about death, it helps to walk myself from the observable fact that dead bodies cease to function to the logical conclusion that dead bodies cease to feel. Will I be able to find that sense of calm when my death seems imminent? I'll let you know. In the meantime, I don't have to worry about earning a spot in the right afterlife. I don't have to worry about which form my spirit will take next. And I don't have to worry about St. Peter.

That's how I deal with my own fears in the face of death.

But—wait—that addresses death only from the point of view of the dead. Addressing death from the point of view of the living is harder.

How do we think about life given that our deaths are inevitable? Religion has a nice fix for this problem too: not only does the afterlife give you life after death, it also gives your earthly life a purpose, whether that purpose is getting into heaven or avoiding eternal hellfire or writing yourself into a Book of Life or moving (in your next incarnation) out of the untouchable caste. But if you're not trying to please God or reach Nirvana, what's the point?

As he got older, this was Jesse's question too.

## WHAT'S THE POINT?

JESSE, AGE ELEVEN, HAD gone to bed happy, with a new book, ten minutes before. Yet here he was in the doorway of the living room about to burst into tears. Delighted as any parent would be at this unscheduled post-bedtime reappearance, I looked at him, raised my eyebrows, and said something comforting, like, "What?" But he didn't stop to explain; he just pitched onto the couch next to me, pressed his head into my side, and sobbed.

I hugged him hard and did a quick mental scan. Was it the new book? No, the book was funny, a cockeyed look at world mythology. Was he anxious about something? There were no recitals or piano competitions on the near horizon. And he had a whole Sunday left before school started again. As far as I knew, life was good. But what did I know?

I let him cry for a few minutes, breathing slowly myself to help his ragged breaths subside, and then I said, "Jess, what's wrong?"

"It's nothing. It's stupid." I waited. "You just die and then it's over," he said. "There's nothing left."

Honestly, I was relieved. This was not some new trauma that required doctors or therapists or internet research in the wee hours. This was an old, familiar topic for us, only now it seemed to have shifted from fear of losing Grandma or fear of being buried to something more abstract: fear of not mattering.

Maybe that humorous book on mythology had for Jesse a brutal subtext: tell whatever stories you want, but that's not going to change what happens in the end. Or maybe the book wasn't enter-taining enough to keep the current of his thoughts rushing, and when that current grew still, the specter of death resurfaced. All I knew was that he had to learn to comfort himself in moments like this—in a real way, a way that would serve him his whole life. It was my job to show him how.

I told Jesse, as I had before, that being dead won't bother us at all, since we'll be dead. I tried to sell the idea of life with no after: no pain, no thoughts, no regrets, nothing.

Yeah, he got that. Still it wasn't enough. "But what's the point?" he said. "If you're just going to disappear?"

Jesse is and was a serious musician. So I started to say that he's less likely to disappear than most people—he'd be leaving behind a haunting nocturne or a great pop album—but then I abandoned the angle, unsure whether achievements really mattered in the grand scheme, or whether, if you step back far enough, those are mean-ingless too. As a writer, I would feel lucky if my work gave someone a moment of pleasure, and luckier still if an idea, a phrase, an argu-ment I made permanently lodged itself in someone's head—at least until *they* die. Eventually, I knew, all my work would disappear.

So what's the point?

"The point is," I said, "to make the most of your life now."

"But it's pointless."

Right, I sighed. "So you might as well enjoy yourself."

This was preaching to the choir, so to speak. Evidence of Jesse's exuberant days filled the house: pages of sheet music in the printer tray, leftover banana bread he'd made on a whim, a penciled list of art projects to do with his sister, ideas for songs scribbled in the first few pages of four different notebooks, and, on the piano (and under the piano and next to the piano), lead sheets for pop songs he was rehearsing with friends.

Jesse lived big. He had big dreams and big talent and big plans; he hugged with his whole body and he sang at full throat; his joy was sunshine happy, and his fury was mine-shaft black.

And occasionally a big wave of grief washed over him when he realized it wasn't going to last forever.

He shrugged off my attempts at reasoned reassurance; he was smart enough to know that there was no answer. That's what he meant when he said, "It's nothing." It's not nothing—it's everything—but there's nothing anyone can do about it.

## MY BIG INSIGNIFICANT AFTERLIFE

IN THE FACE OF their mortality, many people console themselves with the idea that they will be remembered through fame or family. I think that's a losing bet. When my father taught *Hamlet*, he would tell his students to stand up if they knew their parents' first names. Then he would say, "okay, remain standing if you can tell me the first names of all four grandparents." Some kids sat. "Okay," he said, "remain standing if you can tell me the names of all eight great-grandparents." In all his years of teaching, nobody *ever* remained standing past the greats. "Remember me!" harps the Ghost of Hamlet's father. Hamlet does and then he doesn't ("Do not forget," the Ghost is forced to return and remind him) and then he does and then, when Hamlet lies dying, he doesn't mention his dad at all. He says goodbye to his mother and his friend Horatio, selects Fortinbras to replace him, and asks Horatio "to tell my story." The Ghost is ghosted.

Having children is no guarantee of earthly immortality. Eventually, in five acts or five generations, you will be forgotten: your name, your story, you. Some people take a lot of care with their legacies: they make sure to have people and things named after them, and they carefully plot the location of their burying place, the better to be visited in years to come. I hope my children miss me when I die, but only because it will mean they loved me while I lived. Beyond my kids, though? Beyond people whose lives my life has touched? I care no more that my great-grandkids know my name than that they know my dentist's name. I'll be dead, remember?

If I'm being honest, though, I do expect to have an impact on the world. I expect something about me to reverberate. Perhaps I will live on in one of my children's taste for stationery or for salt. In a friend's slightly greater confidence in herself. In the one recipe of all the recipes that a child of mine ends up using, which may or may not be the one recipe of my mother's that I still use. Or maybe in the fact that they eschew all my recipes, believing (like me) that another might be better, so it's better to keep looking.

Here's my fantasy of my afterlife: Every once in a while when my kids are estimating whether a pint or a quart of lentil soup remains in the pot after dinner, they will remember how much I truly loved putting away leftovers and took it as a point of honor to minimize the ullage of each container—and not only that, but how much I loved the word "ullage" (n., the amount by which a container falls short of being full) and other obscure but useful terms. Or maybe they won't remember it came from me at all, they will simply share my ~~compulsion~~ genius. Maybe one of them passes this along to someone else—a kid, a spouse, an amused roommate—and for that person, it won't be a memory of me but a memory of my kid. Or maybe my memorial will be the lentil soup itself, or my habit of making things I don't really like (like lentil soup) to make other people happy, my trick of using baking soda to soften the lentils, my pleasure in revising a recipe after learning a good trick, or my commitment to revision of all kinds. I would pass that one idiosyncrasy along to my children, and they would be conscious of it or not, and then they would pass it along in some form or another—less me, more them—and so on.

(Because this is my fantasy, I left out the bad qualities and habits I am passing on to my kids. For the sake of honesty, though, I hereby bequeath to my daughter, Lena, my faulty, never-repaired body image; to my son Jesse, my perfectionism and fear of looking stupid; to my son Noah, my intolerance for people I find boring. And to each of them I bequeath that cruel thing I said once that I don't remember but that they will never forget. Believe me, my children, if I could keep you from inheriting all this, I would.)

Whatever your circumstances in life, whatever your intentions, the impact of your life reverberates beyond you. So if you need a sense of meaning in your life, you could try making those reverberations more positive than not. In the tiny, mundane ways that I have described, but in larger ones too. Could a novel reverberate? Of course. Could stopping to help a stranger? Standing in the cold to protest a war? Working a double shift in the ER? Yes, all of it.

Even though death looms at the end—even though you yourself will not survive or even be remembered—there's still a point to achieving things in life. When you do big things, your life might reverberate all the more, beyond the people you love, out to strangers, even in future generations.

But I'd hedge my bets by enjoying myself too. Plan for the future if that makes you happy, but revel in the present if you can. Even Epicurus reflected on this duality:

> We must keep in mind that the future is neither completely ours nor not ours, so that we should not fully expect it to come, nor lose hope, as if it were not coming at all.[21]

And so did Setiya, the philosopher, who argued that the key to living life in the face of its inevitable end was combining the telic (goal-oriented) and atelic (non-goal-oriented) dimensions of life—enjoying every moment and not just putting off pleasure and satisfaction until that goal is reached.[22] (After all, you might not reach it. Or you might, and then what do you do?) Not just journey or just destination, but both.

## THERE'S ONE MORE PROBLEM

HOW TO LIVE IN the knowledge that you will one day die is, I'm afraid, only the first problem of death from the point of view of the living.

The second problem is how to live with other people's deaths. Far worse than imagining my own nonexistence is imagining my husband's warm body in bed next to me turning cold, disappearing, evaporating in a cruel time-lapse aerial shot covering—what? Twenty, thirty, forty more years if we're lucky. Blink of an historical eye. Here and then gone. Smelling of sweat and woodsmoke and apple and then gone. Whistling in the shower, drumrolling down stairs, centering my life, and then gone.

When my friend's daughter died, I made myself picture the loss of my own little girl. The way she stood on a chair at the kitchen counter and said, eyes twinkling, finger in the butter dish, "Can I have a taste of butter?" Gone. The way she sat in her booster seat and pretended to talk to her daddy on the phone, saying, "Well, sorry, we just left the grocery, you should have called before." Gone. The way she'd hold my cheeks and kiss me eight times and then ask, "How many times was that?" Gone. Her rounded tummy, gone, her muscled legs, gone, her brown bangs, gone. Her little fingers on which she proudly displayed fingernails *not bitten*. All gone.

Would I want to believe she still existed somewhere if she didn't anymore? I guess, if I really thought I would see her again, I would. But mostly I would want her back. *Want her back. Want her back.* I would never not want her back, never not want to go back to the day before I lost her. I would only, maybe, years later, learn not to think about it as much.

The strange thing is, as I write, when she's now sixteen years old, crocheting in her bedroom (floor made of unfolded laundry, walls made of fandom and feminism), I still want that little girl back. I love Lena as she is now, and I love being her mother now. My only complaint is with the passage of time. I will never again hold—and indeed I am frighteningly beginning to forget—the girl who said "fweater" for sweater, who matched striped tights with a striped shirt and a flower-print skirt. The four-year-old is gone. The seven-year-old is gone, too, the one who dressed like a teen pop star, the one who—while her big brother fought his fear of death—begged to get out of the car and look at the dead squirrel in the road. The one who was fascinated by car crashes and Renaissance paintings of saints suffering their gory fates.

Today's Lena distracts me from the loss of yesterday's, but still I feel the loss. Not the death of my child but the death of her childhood. This sense of loss is of a different order of magnitude, of course: a faint ache rather than what I imagine would be searing, breathtaking pain. I wouldn't even mention them together—oh, my dear old friend, forgive me—except that I believe the answer to both kinds of loss is the same: to live as well as one can and love as well as one can right this minute.

᭟

Ten minutes after Jesse, age eleven, despaired of the pointlessness of life in the face of death, the wave of grief passed. When he headed back to bed, it occurred to me that, rather than getting up in the first place, he could have stayed there, alone, and cried himself to sleep. That's what I would have done. That's what I did do, as a child, when I was suddenly struck with the thought that my parents would die. Instead, Jesse got up to tell me how he was feeling, to give and receive a long hug, to hear my voice. Making his sorrow—every human's sorrow—a moment of connection rather than isolation.

I didn't know for sure how to face death, either, but it seemed to me that he was getting it.

# HOW TO START YOUR OWN HOLIDAY

*A life without a holiday is like a long journey*
*without an inn to rest at.*

DEMOCRITUS

D O YOU REMEMBER WHAT you did for dinner last October 12? Don't look or guess—just try to remember. No? How about last Thanksgiving?

That's my twenty-four-word argument in favor of holidays. Without holidays, the past dissolves into a smooth blur. With them, our brains can hold on at least to a few moments from the past. And with them, our brains have places to grasp as they climb the sheer rock face of the future.

I never appreciated this more urgently than during the early Covid Era, when our calendars were wiped clean along with every conceivable surface, an erasure as disconcerting as the lockdown itself. The horizon that normally rose and dipped and beckoned with recitals and travel and graduations was now smooth as a cartoon moon, and equally uninviting. Even the gentle undulations of the weekly routine had vanished. Gone were the rehearsals that made Sundays Sunday, the town board meetings that made Wednesdays Wednesday. Dates that never change had changed, and events that always happened were canceled: the NBA playoffs, the Eurovision Song Contest, even Wimbledon for the first time since World War II.

Less than three weeks into this new, featureless, futureless reality, this interminable *present*, I joined my parents and sisters for a
virtual Shabbat.

As you know, we celebrated the Jewish sabbath when I was a
kid with a family dinner on Friday evenings. We did not take the
religion part very seriously, but we were pretty committed to the
holiday part—the weekly observance of it. Shabbat dinner made
Fridays Friday in my childhood home.

Some features of time's landscape are temporary. When my
daughter played the oboe, Sundays eddied around midday wind-en-
semble rehearsals, but they don't anymore. For now, the second
Wednesday of the month means town board meetings for Adam,
but he won't serve forever. Religious holidays are, by contrast, re-
assuringly permanent. Even if a state of emergency has temporar-
ily closed the church's doors, Easter is always going to be when
Easter is (the first Sunday after the first full moon after the vernal
equinox). The parades may be canceled, but not St. Patrick's Day.

The same goes for the sabbath. Jews have been officially resting on the seventh day for thousands of years; that fact wasn't
going to change just because during the lockdown we were also
"resting" on all six previous days. So even though in pre-pandemic times we wouldn't have gotten together—or even called
each other—and even though in pre-pandemic times none of our
families kept the sabbath anymore, we agreed to meet on what
the calendar said was Friday and try to make it *feel* like Friday by
lighting candles and saying prayers. We lifted martini glasses for
the prayer over the wine, my father added an extra blessing for
Purell, and no one except my big sister remembered to bless the
bread. But still, it helped. Religion had given us a date that real
life couldn't easily delete.

Holidays may seem like one of religion's more frivolous perks,
like Renaissance paintings or organ music, but they have a way of
anchoring our lives that we might not appreciate until we attempt
to give them up. We need them more than we think we do. So

here's where I tell you exactly how to replace all the holidays that your official rejection of God will prevent you from observing.

Actually, no. Sorry. It's more complicated than that.

## A CHRISTMAS STORY

DRIVING LENA TO PRESCHOOL in mid-December:

"Why don't *we* decorate for Christmas?"

"Well, how would you want to decorate?"

"Why don't we have a Christmas tree? Maxie has a Christmas tree." Max was Lena's oldest brother's best friend; he had the authority of a big brother crossed with the celebrity of not being in our family. He did, indeed, have a Christmas tree, which we usually got to help decorate.

"Well, okay . . . Here's the thing . . . Christmas *seems* like it's just about trees and presents and lights and stuff, but it's really a holiday that celebrates somebody's birthday. He lived a long time ago, his name is Jesus, and a lot of people think he was God, but we don't think he was, so we don't celebrate his birthday."

*What?* (sputtered the argument inside my head). Why would you have to think someone was a god to celebrate his birthday? Have you ever heard of Martin Luther King? Or Grandma? Does *Max* think Jesus was God? His parents' background was Christian, but what did *they* actually believe?

Fortunately, my elementary school logicians were not in the car, just the preschool pragmatist. She was silent for a moment. Then she asked, of Jesus, "Did he die?"

"Yes."

"How did he die?"

"Some people killed him."

"But how? Did they shoot him?"

"No. Do you really want to know? It's kind of gross."

"Yes."

I knew she meant it.

"They nailed him to a cross and let him hang up there until he died." Truthfully, I was never exactly sure what killed Jesus. Thirst? Blood loss? Heart attack? Tetanus?

But Lena appeared to accept the inherently fatal properties of being nailed to a cross. Except, "What's a cross?"

"It's a big wooden . . . it's shaped like a little *t* and sticks up from the ground . . . I'll show you a picture."

"How old was he when he died?"

"Thirty-three, I think."

"But if he was a grown-up, why didn't he run away?"

That made me sad—the child's assumption that all grown-ups have power over their lives. And, of course, the part of the story she didn't know yet: that, as a god, he could have run away but chose not to. Or at least he could have renounced his own teachings. But he didn't. That is the crucial element of the Christian story and the poignant aspect of the human story, which together made up what was, I had to admit, a pretty durable and compelling myth.

Whether Jesus was a completely fictional character or a historical character whose talents have been exaggerated, he wasn't a bad character.

> When you give a luncheon or a dinner, do not invite your friends or your brothers or your relatives or rich neighbors, in case they may invite you in return, and you would be repaid. But when you give a banquet, invite the poor, the crippled, the lame, and the blind. (Luke 14:12–13)

> If you wish to be perfect, go, sell your possessions, and give the money to the poor. (Matthew 19:21)

So why not celebrate his birthday?

We did when I was a kid, even though both my parents were

Jewish. And they had each celebrated Christmas when they were kids, even though both sets of their parents on both sides were Jewish too. My mom had been raised Reform Jewish in Atlanta, and my dad was from a Sephardic Jewish family in Montgomery. His father had, according to legend, spread fake snow in front of their fireplace, into which he pressed "Santa's" footprints. In my own childhood home, on December 23 or 24, we decorated our Christmas tree with lights, tinsel (always griped about, always used), and homemade ornaments, some preserved from my mother's childhood trees. On top: a foil-covered Star of David. Tacked to the mantel over the fireplace: stockings embroidered by my father's mother, the child of Russian Jewish immigrants. Under the tree: a trove of presents. Christmas morning was pj's, wrapping paper, and a note from Santa in my father's calligraphy thanking us for the cookies we had left him.

Although I had nothing but happy memories of Christmas in my childhood home, I did not attempt to re-create them for my own children. Had I strictly renounced the celebration of all holidays in whose origins I didn't believe? No, I had not. After all, we celebrated Chanukah.

Chanukah is an eight-day festival that (in brief, and arguably) commemorates a second-century BCE victory of Jewish rebels against the Seleucid Empire, a Greek state that had banned Jewish practice and seized the Second Temple of Jerusalem. When the victorious rebels re-entered the Temple to reconsecrate it, they found only one day's worth of oil, which miraculously lasted the eight days it took to replenish the supply. That was God's doing, of course, and, according to the song "Rock of Ages" (which I made my kids sing before they could open their presents), his "saving power" was responsible for the military victories as well: "furious, they assailed us / but Thine arm availed us." The story has a human hero too: Judah, the son of the priest who led the rebellion. Judah was called Judah the Hammer—Judah Maccabee—because he was unusually ferocious in battle.

He destroyed every male by the edge of the sword, and razed
and plundered the town. Then he passed through the town
over the bodies of the dead. (1 Maccabees 5:51)

And so on. It's a bloody story.

Lena *should* have asked, "Why do we celebrate Chanukah?" but
she didn't. Possibly she knew that if I followed my lack of belief to
its logical conclusion, she would have thereafter been deprived of
that one good and seven "um, thanks" presents she got every year.
Or maybe children don't think to question the good things in their
lives. If she *had* asked why we celebrated Chanukah, I would have
had to tell her that it was her fault. Without kids, we would have
been perfectly happy to let the cobwebs grow on the wedding-pres-
ent menorahs. But *with* kids, choosing to abstain from a culturally
(if not religiously) appropriate present-giving holiday would be,
well, Scrooge-ish. In that sense, we were bowing our heads not so
much to God but to American consumer culture, version Jew.0.

In religious terms, Chanukah is a minor holiday, but its place
on the calendar pits it against Christmas, which makes it seem bigger than it is—or at least inspires North American Jews to use it
as a sort of consolation prize. But since we believed the roots of
both holidays were equally fictional, and the timing of each was
suspiciously convenient for adding light to a dark season, why *not*
choose the holiday with the great songs, the blinged-out tree, and
the cute baby?

Or why not celebrate both, as I had as a child? Why had Adam
and I adopted a strict guest-privileges-only attitude toward Christmas, in which we could help Max decorate his tree, but we never
had our own? The answer was obvious, although, as usual, it took
my daughter to say it out loud. When, under her relentless pester-
ing and my own self-questioning, I started to waver—"Well, maybe
we *could* do Christmas in our own way. Have our own tradition"—
she pinpointed the problem: "But Grandpa would get mad."

Ah. Let's just say Adam's family definitely didn't celebrate Christmas when he was growing up. The thought of Grandpa seeing a Christmas tree in his grandchildren's house made me shiver.

"We wouldn't have to tell Grandpa."

"Mom"—she said, in the key of *duh*—"I think he would find out."

"How?"

"All the decorations!"

Naturally. What would be the point of a low-key Christmas? Did I not understand the word "celebrate"?

## HOLY DAY OR HOLLOW DAY?

I KNOW A LOT of people who don't believe in God. But off the top of my head, I can't think of any—not one—who doesn't celebrate a religious holiday in some way. I doubt I'll ever completely stop. Even beyond the marking of time, they can be useful. Although I didn't believe God was actually the Rock of Ages, I could *use* Chanukah to celebrate the miracle of having light during dark months or hope in times of despair. Although I didn't believe in the Burning Bush, I could use Passover to celebrate the fight against oppression. Although I didn't believe Jesus was the son of God, I could use Christmas to celebrate the idea of peace and self-sacrifice. Emptied of their serious religious content, these holidays could be filled with my own moral, political, or philosophical ideas.

But I still wouldn't find them completely satisfying. German philosopher Josef Pieper would probably say that's because a hollowed-out holy day is just that—hollow—no matter how well I decorate, or explicate. His *In Tune with the World: A Theory of Festivity* argues that believing in the gods that inspired a religious holiday is essential to celebrating it fully. To him, you can't truly celebrate Christmas if the birth of Jesus means nothing to you. "If the incarnation of God is no longer understood as an event

that directly concerns the present lives of men," he writes, "it becomes impossible, even absurd, to celebrate Christmas festively."[1]
It would be a cheap imitation of the real thing, all wrapping and no
gift. Same with Carnival, the Catholic festive season before Lent:
"Carnival remains festive," he says, "only where Ash Wednesday
still exists."[2] A bit pompous, but I take his point. You can throw
beads and get drunk and march in a parade, but without Lent and
sacrifice looming (and Christ's sacrifice underlying that), it's just
empty fun. I think that's what I have intuited in the past when I
felt I couldn't attend the Break the Fast celebration that follows
Yom Kippur without having fasted. No one would know, of course,
if I had eaten that day or not, and obviously I didn't think that
God was watching, but without fasting, the meal of bagels, lox,
and quiche would be just a meal. Only after fasting does the meal
become a feast.

But not even fasting felt like enough to make Yom Kippur feel
real. Once, as we were approaching the holiday, an adolescent
Noah said to me casually, "I think I'll fast on Wednesday."

"Oh, really? Why?"

"Aren't we going to a Break the Fast at Grandpa's?"

"Yeah."

"Well, I want to be really hungry."

"Are you also going to be thinking about all the ways you could
try to be better this year? 'Cause that's kind of the point."

"Nah, I'm not doing that."

Can you hear the disdainful teenager? Can you hear the frus-
trated mom? It's not that I wanted him to be religious; it's that I
didn't want him to do the outer part without the inner part—the
ritual without the meaning, the holiday without the "holy."

Most years on Yom Kippur, I did try to heed the religious cue
to spend my day reassessing my behavior over the past twelve
months. But did the Day of Atonement ever give me, a nonbeliever, the sense of soul-cleansing at-oneness with the world that
a believer might feel? I don't think so. Celebrating the holidays of

religions I don't believe in gives me *something*, but not the whole thing. It's as if I heard the distant beat of music or saw two people in love. Pieper may decry my participation in religious holidays as "sham practicing"[3]; I think of it as sidling up close to something I desire but cannot have.

What exactly do I desire, though? A true holiday, says Pieper, is a brief period when the everyday thins to transparency and we can see through and underneath it the wondrous, incredible, beauteous gift of this world and our lives in it. When we celebrate a holiday, "suddenly the walls of the solid here and now are burst asunder and the everyday realm of existence is thrown open to eternity."[4] Yes, that. We pause, we see, we rejoice. That's what I want.

## OKAY, THEN, I'LL JUST MAKE ONE UP

I LOVE PIEPER'S LITTLE book because his respect for holidays—his conviction that they can resonate on a deep level—matches my own. But I don't agree with him that religion is the only possible source of resonance. To Pieper, "praise of the world" is the essential feature of a holiday. And since he assumes the world was created by God, he declares that every true holiday must have at its core the recognition of the divine. That would leave me permanently on the outside, looking in. But we can praise creation without praising a creator. We just might have to make up our own holiday to do it.

We begin with a suitable occasion. A holiday can't be totally random—that's just a party. At the same time, firm dates on the calendar with no personal significance won't do, either. Anyone who has essentially ignored (or just gone shopping on) President's Day understands what Pieper means by "the pallor of the merely 'legal' holidays."[5] A holiday has to repeat, but it can't *only* repeat. It has to mean something.

We tried a few different things in our house. For a while when the kids were young and summers meant solo parenting while Adam, a farmer, got the hay in, I instituted Adventure Saturday, a variation on a sabbath. The idea was that every Saturday the kids and I had to do something none of us had ever done before: a new museum, new hike, new food. In terms of providing a break in the unending ennui that was caring for young children and giving us things to remember, discuss, and look forward to, Adventure Saturday was a festal success. It was a success, too, in terms of guilt release: because of Adventure Saturday, I could allow myself *Blue's Clues* Tuesday and Mom-Ignores-You Monday and Same-Old-Playground Sunday. One day of enrichment excused six days of just getting by. I believe this is a little-discussed advantage of suffering holidays like Lent and Yom Kippur and Ramadan. You don't have to be good *all* the time as long as you know you'll be good at this particular time. Did we pause, see, and rejoice? Sometimes we did.

But Adventure Saturday tapered off as the children got older and busier and not as desperately tedious to be alone in the house with. In *For Small Creatures Such as We*, Sasha Sagan writes about her made-up holiday tradition, Ladies Dining Society, which met once a month for years until too many friends scattered too far to sustain the tradition. "Just as easily as these traditions fall away, new ones can begin," she writes. "There's nothing to stop you from writing to your friends today and trying something new."[6] For a while, we celebrated a holiday called School's Out. (If you don't give your holiday a name, you're not even trying.) Most people get excited about the last day of school—even I did, despite the fact that, a mere seventy-three hours into summer vacation, someone in our house was sure to be poking holes in the couch upholstery out of desperate, full-body boredom. Nevertheless, every year we celebrated with a meal of French fries, nachos, margaritas (for some of us), and—this is the crucial bit—no fruit or vegetables. Nothing healthy whatsoever, because, hey, School's Out!

That was a glorious holiday, but short-lived. Once I could see that my children were reasonably healthy and liked broccoli, my food rules relaxed, and the absolute sacred/profane glory of the fried and the cheesy faded. School's Out was always doomed, in any case, tied as it was to an academic calendar that at some point would not pertain.

After Jesse became a vegetarian, I insisted that we celebrate his Veggiversary (with French fries *and* broccoli) because I was proud of him for sticking with it. It's June 8; you can send him a card. But honestly, I've stopped trying to come up with new holidays since we accidentally arrived at one that is almost perfect.

## INTERNATIONAL PIZZA DAY

WHEN NOAH WAS FIVE, we read a picture book by Nancy Castaldo called *Pizza for the Queen*, which told the story of the invention of pizza Margherita. It ends with a recipe and a note: "If you need a reason to have a slice of pizza, February 9 has been declared International Pizza Day."[7]

It happened to be February 4. I decided to celebrate International Pizza Day that year not because I thought it would become a new family holiday, but because I was trying to be spontaneous and do stuff with my kids—especially stuff that started in a book and ended in the kitchen. It's not like I was going to build them a treehouse. Making a pizza I could manage. So I said, "Hey, we should celebrate!" and on February 9 we made pizzas, each of us choosing our own toppings. Later we mentioned International Pizza Day to two friends, who insisted they be invited next time. The year after that, they wrote a song, whose verses multiplied along with our guest list.

Although I had no grand plan to introduce a new secular holiday into our household, International Pizza Day just sort of worked. So in the tradition of all the best how-tos, I will extract a few precepts from our experience and pretend I knew what I was doing the whole time.

**1. Use a holiday that already exists.** This is a time-honored technique. Did you know, for instance, that December 25 was when the Romans celebrated a holiday called Dies Natalis Solis Invicti, the Day of the Birth of the Unconquered Sun? The word "Easter" comes from Eostre, who was a Germanic goddess of spring and rebirth, which might explain the bunnies and eggs that oddly accompany the (more recent) celebration of Jesus's resurrection. This isn't laziness; it's strategy. When Pope Gregory sent missionaries to convert the Anglo Saxons in 596, he recommended rechristening, so to speak, the holidays the locals were already celebrating:

> Let them therefore, on the day of the dedication of their churches, or on the feast of the martyrs whose relics are preserved in them, build themselves huts around their one-time temples and celebrate the occasion with religious feasting.[8]

As Sagan writes, "New cultures are so often built on old cultures."[9] So go ahead and use an established holiday or event and make it your own. Here's where we could use President's Day, or some other holiday that has come into our calendars or our consciousness without religion attached, from the silly (Pi Day, May the Fourth) to the pointed (Darwin Day). You could come up with family traditions to mark Pride Month or Women's History Month. Or you could smoke weed with your friends at 4:20 p.m. on April 20 and think about the oneness of the universe.

International Pizza Day was mentioned in the back of a children's book—just a date, really, with no explanation other than the "coincidence" of its also being the author's birthday. I'm all for recycling.

**2. Pick an organizing theme with universal and eternal appeal.** Who can resist a magical baby born in a barn? Who doesn't hope that the new year is better than the old one? Who doesn't love *pizza* in some form or other? For long-term durability, make sure your festival doesn't have an expiration date (such as the moment your children age out of the academic calendar). But it's okay if it's mundane: remember, holidays are a special day to celebrate the ordinary, to praise the world and our good fortune to be in it (eating pizza). Pieper again:

> Whenever we happen to feel heartfelt assent, to find that something specific is good, wonderful, glorious, rapturous—a drink of fresh water, the precise functioning of a tool, the colors of a landscape, the charm of a loving gesture, a poem [or the perfect ratio of sauce to cheese to crust], our praise always reaches beyond the given object . . . Our tribute always contains at least a smattering of affirmation of the world, as a whole.[10]

**3. Establish traditional foods.** Choose something you crave but don't eat often: Latkes. King cake. Eggnog. For International Pizza Day, we had to overcome the fact that pizza is, shall we say, relatively common. So our guests add toppings to their individual prebaked crusts, and then we bake each pizza over the course of the evening, which may or may not feature a smoke alarm and hasty midwinter ventilation due to the volatile meeting of mozzarella grease and 550-degree clay tiles. We may eat pizza once a week in normal life, but only on IPD do we eat charred sourdough pizza with (say) spinach, gorgonzola, and caramelized onions in a smoky room after a solid ninety minutes of waiting our turn.

**4. Embrace extravagance.** Holidays are marked in part by "absence of calculation, in fact, lavishness," writes Pieper. And anyone who's made a wary, full-belly approach to the Thanksgiving dessert table knows "extravagance that violates all rationality"[11] is still achievable in our world of plenty. It doesn't have to be the feasting that's extravagant, though; you can also travel far, spend too much, wear clothes you wear only once a year, or make amends for each and every harm you have caused. A marathon could be made into a holiday, as could an annual hike or a relay reading of *Mrs. Dalloway*. Running twenty-six miles to no purpose, climbing a peak just to climb down again, or reading a book out loud instead of working or sleeping—any behavior that goes far beyond the everyday. Our pizza-topping table includes a vegan section, two kinds of olives, three kinds of sausage, garlic confit, and béchamel spiked with parmesan. It's out of control.

Does preparing all those toppings sound like a lot of work? Exactly. This, I believe, is the surprise secret step:

**5. Make sure your holiday is a pain in the ass.** Here are some examples of holidays with the requisite pain-in-the-ass quotient: The one where you have to buy presents for everyone, cut down a tree, prop the tree up in your house, and cover it with decorations. The one where, for a whole month, you don't eat while the sun is shining. The one where you have to dispose of all the yeast-friendly food in your house, change all your plates and silverware, and, for a week, eat nothing containing grains or beans.

A true holiday isn't just something to look forward to; it's also something to dread. It should loom in the distance like a storm that promises to leave in its wake both indelible memories and a terrible mess. Sacrifice is key. "In voluntarily keeping the holiday, men renounce the yield of a day's labor," writes Pieper. "As the animal for sacrifice was taken from the herd, so a piece of available time was expressly withdrawn from utility."[12] I'll say. I give up a week every year for IPD. We tried to celebrate during the pandemic—just four of us were home—but we ate crusts from the freezer that had been left over from the year before and made do with the toppings we keep in store. Which meant that instead of celebrating IPD, we were . . . eating pizza for dinner. It wasn't just the absence of guests that deflated the day; it was the absence of labor. The labor is enormous, extravagant, extreme. Every year, the number of crusts I make in advance gets larger, and every year, my husband suggests we order in. This is ritual, too, and I ritually scoff. Because I know that if we made it easy, International Pizza Day would cease to be.

**6. Take your holiday seriously, or no one else will.** "Holiday" comes from "Holy Day," remember. Any good holiday contains an element of "always," that mysteriously powerful substance that can cast a warm and happy glow on, for example, basement accommodations and nonstop dishwashing. If you honor the "always" of your holiday and insist that others do, too, with time and conviction you can get your parents to plan their work schedules around driving eight hours just to eat a half-burned pizza that they had to make themselves. Prepare a pained and puzzled look in case a friend makes alternate plans on the weekend of your new holiday. Practice saying, "But it's *[name of holiday]*!" the way an Irish matriarch might say, "But it's *St. Patrick's Day*!" When a teenage child begs to volunteer at a hospital that morning, shake your head slowly and say, "I don't know, honey. It's [name of holiday]. Are you sure they need you?"

**7. No, really, take it seriously.** Pause, see, rejoice. International Pizza Day is frivolous and fun and hectic and exhausting, but it is real. It celebrates things my family holds dear: welcoming guests, cooking food from scratch, being serious about silly things, mixing generations, and making an effort. It celebrates the alchemy of turning cheap things into luxurious ones: onions cooked down to sweet golden threads; flour, water, and oil transformed into chewy, tangy crusts. At the end of every IPD, after I have baked the last pizza, I take off my apron and stand on a chair in the packed dining room to read "The Miracle of the Pizza," a pseudo-biblical story in which it seems there won't be enough flour to make all the pizza crusts, but somehow, there is.

> And so it was, that by a mere two tablespoons of King Arthur Unbleached All-Purpose Flour, peace reigned in the household.

And it was good.

May the toppings multiply and the cheese melt evenly in the
oven, Now and forever . . .

The scripture may be a spoof, but believe me when I tell you
that it is with genuine, not to say religious, fervor that everyone in
that room concludes, "Amen."

**8. Make it "real."** Each of my children had to do a second-grade
project on a family tradition. The point was inclusivity: a good
teacher was making sure that everyone in class got a chance to show
off their cultures. Even so, and even though my children loved International Pizza Day, I was not able to convince a single one of
them to feature homemade pizza and toppings on their poster
board display. "No, Mom," they'd say. "It has to be a *real* holiday."
That is to say, a *holiday celebrated outside our house.*

This, my friends, Step 8, is why I said that IPD was "almost"
perfect. Making up your own private holiday is deeply satisfying,
but also, inevitably, disappointingly *private.* "True festivals . . .
include rapture, oblivion of ills, a sense of harmony with the
world,"[13] writes Pieper, and I think he means finding harmony
with the World—the universal—by rejoicing in the eternals of
host and guest, food and drink, fire and substance, and even the
cyclical return (and blessed departure) of February. But there's
also the world you live in, and it is a glorious thing to feel a sense
of harmony with that.

Which is why, despite myself, despite IPD, despite nonbelief, I
keenly sympathized with Lena's desire for Christmas. Some people
hate that it cannot be avoided, but that's what I love about the holiday. Everyone seems to be doing something Christmas-related on
December 24 and 25, be it fighting for parking at the mall, nailing
stockings to a mantel, or sitting down at a Chinese restaurant with
other Jews. Whether you crave Christmas music or can't stand it,

in the US, at least, you are unlikely to escape it entirely. You still have to go to the grocery store.

Raising children only increases your contact with the prevailing culture's biggest holiday. We've never sent our kids to school on December 25. Think about that. Even the Jewish Community Center preschool closes for Christmas. Every year we went to Christmas concerts in which our children's secular chorus performed holiday songs. We gave presents to all the kids' teachers because "the holidays" are a time to express your appreciation. We attended holiday parties in classrooms decorated in Christmas-tree green and Santa-suit red.

I could have resented my forced participation in a holiday that didn't actually include me. Instead, I took from it what I could. I made a production out of home-baked teacher presents, and I made a point of stuffing cash into every Salvation Army bucket. I played Bing Crosby and Burl Ives of my own accord, and I had my own stash of star, bell, and reindeer-shaped cookie cutters.

On Christmas, I revel in that glorious sense of being in tune with the world around me. But I wonder how it would feel to believe in the Nativity.

On International Pizza Day, I revel in being in tune with the World as I see it, when my everyday realm of existence is thrown open to eternity. But I wish that the world around me—not just our party guests, but everyone—could share in that joy.

## IN TUNE WITH THE WORLD

THERE IS ONE COMMONLY celebrated American holiday that I do believe in: Thanksgiving. I'm not talking about the whitewashed and irredeemably racist "First Thanksgiving" I learned about in elementary school—the one where pilgrims and Indians feasted amicably together in mutual respect and mutually beneficial coexistence. But the origins of the federal holiday lie elsewhere. We can (and should) discard that myth without discarding Thanksgiving.

Thank goodness. Since I was a child, Thanksgiving has been my favorite holiday, the one that my family of origin takes the most seriously, for which my parents do the most preparing and have the highest expectation of family participation.

Although Thanksgiving is a secular holiday, celebrated both by nonbelievers and by believers of different faiths, its origins are admittedly religious. Apparently, New England colonists used to declare days of prayer in which to give thanks to God, and George Washington's Thanksgiving proclamation—October 3, 1789—does just that. It recommends "a day of public thanksgiving and prayer to be . . . devoted by the People of these States to the service of that great and glorious Being, who is the beneficent Author of all the good that was, that is, or that will be."

Okay, got it. No wiggle room there. From "Whereas" to "in the year of our Lord 1789," in 456 words, there are seven mentions of God as a noun, four as a pronoun, and five as a possessive adjective. Where's the food? The feast? The harvest? One word—"plenty"—will have to suffice.

The official holiday as we know it today, celebrated at the time of year we now celebrate it, began seventy-four years later. Abraham Lincoln's Thanksgiving Proclamation opens like this: "The year that is drawing towards its close, has been filled with the blessings of fruitful fields and healthful skies." Ah, that's more like it. But—wait—that's shocking! The year that was drawing to a close was 1863, the bloodiest year of the Civil War. Those fruitful fields were the scenes of gruesome, relentless slaughter: more than one hundred thousand soldiers were killed or injured in the battles of Gettysburg, Chancellorsville, and Chickamauga alone. This would be like writing, mid-September 2001, "It's been another beautiful week in New York City."

But that's the point of this call for gratitude: we have cause to give thanks even in the midst of our great national horror. Lincoln's proclamation—probably written by his secretary of state,

William Seward—is longer than Washington's and refers to God less often but does so far more pointedly: "No human counsel hath devised nor hath any mortal hand worked out these great things. They are the gracious gifts of the Most High God . . ." It goes on:

> To these bounties, which are so constantly enjoyed that we are prone to forget the source from which they come, others have been added, which are of so extraordinary a nature, that they cannot fail to penetrate and soften even the heart which is habitually insensible to the ever watchful providence of Almighty God.

I remain, of course, irredeemably insensible to the providence of Almighty God, but I do believe in the gracious gifts that I enjoy, and I acknowledge that I am liable, like most people, to forget my own good fortune. I am grateful to have that reminder on my calendar, the annual injunction to return to the Shenandoah Valley, to golden-green farms and glinting creeks and my parents' love. To me, Thanksgiving means them, it means us, but it means even more because all across the country, people are doing the same thing. Battling traffic, bearing cookies, bickering maybe, but being reminded all over again how lucky they are. Lincoln again:

> It has seemed to me fit and proper that [these gifts] should be solemnly, reverently and gratefully acknowledged as with one heart and one voice by the whole American People. I do therefore invite my fellow citizens in every part of the United States, and also those who are at sea and those who are sojourning in foreign lands, to set apart and observe the last Thursday of November next, as a day of Thanksgiving and Praise.

Most of us do, in one way or another. And I love that. Whenever someone (my husband) suggests we take turkey off the menu in favor of some entrée that everyone actually craves, I rebuff the idea.

Because what I crave is knowing that an enormous number of my fellow Americans are struggling, like me, to figure out how to produce turkey with moist breast meat, crispy skin, and fully cooked thighs. What I crave is knowing that we are, in kitchens across America, almost in unison, making some kind of potato dish and possibly three. What I crave is joining my own heart and voice to everyone else's, to be, for a day, both in tune with the world around me and in tune with the World inside me. What I crave is a day in which everyday foods—dinner rolls!—rise to a higher significance, and because of which there is something already on the calendar to look forward to (and dread) next year. There's no divine miracle at the core of this holiday and no scripture. Just a table to be filled with food and surrounded with celebrants and a day in which to pause, see, and rejoice.

# HOW WILL WE KNOW
# RIGHT FROM WRONG?

*One is often told that it is a very wrong thing to attack
religion, because religion makes one virtuous.
So I am told; I have not noticed it.*

BERTRAND RUSSELL, "Why I Am Not a Christian"

I
F MORTALITY IS WHY people want to believe in God, morality is why people think they should. As philosopher Daniel
Dennett writes, most people "believe in belief in God,"[1] whether
or not they themselves actually believe in God, because they want
to be good, and they think that's where morality comes from. Our
laws and customs share that assumption, from the tradition of having witnesses swear on a Bible to the seven state constitutions bar-
ring atheists from holding public office. Why does belief in God
make you tell the truth or serve reliably as a public servant? It's
simple. Only a person who believes in God, according to the state
of Maryland, believes that he "will be held morally accountable for
his acts, and be rewarded or punished therefore either in this world
or in the world to come."[2] Pennsylvania, too, equates believing in
God with having moral guardrails; it doesn't mention atheists but
explicitly welcomes any officeholder "who acknowledges the being
of a God and a future state of rewards and punishments."[3] The
presumption is that belief in God makes people behave.

These codes were ruled unconstitutional more than sixty years
ago,[4] and attempts to invoke them are rare. But they're worth men-
tioning because (1) they are still on the books and (2) people still
believe that religious adherence equates to morality. A 2020 Pew

survey found that 44 percent of Americans thought you had to believe in God to be moral.[5] In 2019, then–Attorney General William
Barr blamed "moral chaos" and a host of social ills, real and imagined, on the secular rejection of "a real, transcendent moral order
which flows from God's eternal law."[6] More recently, one politician
argued for posting the Ten Commandments in Alabama schools by
insisting, "We've got an entire generation that has no earthly idea
of what's right and what's wrong."[7] A Republican Congressman
sought to blame the massacre in Uvalde, Texas, on the left, which,
he said, had "taken God out of the classroom."[8]

It's not just the right wing, though. Martin Luther King Jr.
said that you could tell whether a law was just or unjust by asking
whether it aligned with God's law: "A man-made code that squares
with the moral law, or the law of God, is a just law."[9] Here he presents "moral law" and "law of God" as synonyms. Martin Luther
King Jr. was a pastor, it's true. But you don't have to be religious to
believe religion is essential to morality or, conversely, that a non-
believer is more likely to be immoral. In a 2017 study, researchers
found that even atheists presume serial killers are more likely to be
atheist than not.[10]

For the record, self-described atheists and humanists made up a
grand total of 0.1 percent of the federal prison population in 2021.[11]
But why do so many people *think* religion is the source of morality? And where does morality come from if not from "God's eternal
law"? How *do* we figure out what laws are just or not? Without the
Ten Commandments on our classroom walls, where do we learn
right from wrong? How do we know what to teach our children—
and what to think ourselves—about how to treat one another?

## PASSOVER AND THE DEAD BABIES

WHEN OUR KIDS WERE little, Adam and I would go to my in-
laws' house for the Passover seder, the annual celebration of the

Israelites' escape from slavery in Egypt. We didn't believe that God was responsible for that escape (and we weren't totally sure whether there really *had been* an escape to be grateful for), but we did believe in the blessings of family harmony and of having someone else cook dinner. And I, at least, believed that Passover was a good opportunity to teach the kids some Big Lessons about oppression, slavery, and freedom. About how people should treat other people.

But first: the Big Lesson about patience. Passover seders are famously long affairs. "Seder" means order: all the steps of the ceremony have to be completed in sequence. There are fifteen steps; dinner is number eleven. So there's a long time between seating and eating Grandma's matzo ball soup, long enough for us all to empathize with the Israelites and their forty years of scrounging in the desert. By the time you get to eat matzo—step seven—even the sand-dry "bread of affliction" tastes like manna from heaven.

So as a dutiful daughter-in-law, a determined parent, and a good student, I arrived prepared with everything the internet had to offer to distract children who were suffering through a seder: crosswords, word searches, and color-your-own cartoons of the ten plagues that God sends to Egypt, when Pharaoh keeps refusing to let his people go. What child could resist the fun of crayoning pictures of lice, flies, boils, locusts, and frogs—especially frogs, the fun plague? Right?

But no matter how many coloring pages I waved around, my children fixated, outraged, on the dead babies. There is a lot of baby killing in the Moses story, beginning with the Egyptian edict that all the Hebrew baby boys be thrown into the Nile and ending with God sending the Angel of Death to kill all non-Jewish firstborn children. Why, my children wanted to know, did so many babies have to die?

Remember: I was raising atheists. They had never been to synagogue or church. They did not know the Ten Commandments, much less the 613 commandments of the Mosaic law. They had not studied Sharia; they had not heard of the Beatitudes. Still, somehow, they got the notion that killing babies was wrong. I certainly didn't intend to convince them otherwise. But maybe instead of trying to justify or explain away the infanticide, I could dig further into the demoralizing effects of slavery and reframe the carnage as the tragic collateral damage of oppression.

I wasn't alone in my quest to recontextualize the story of Exodus. Many Reform and reform-minded Jews focus their seders on what they see as the antislavery, pro-liberation elements of the Passover story. *The Freedom Seder*, published in the wake of Martin Luther King Jr.'s assassination, was the first to relate the overthrow of the Egyptians to the American struggles for abolition and civil rights, but most modern Haggadot—seder guidebooks—that I've encountered at least gesture to the universal struggle between oppressor and oppressed.

Following their lead and my own liberal inclinations, I found quotes from Harriet Tubman and Frederick Douglass. I found a recording of Paul Robeson singing "Go Down, Moses." Technically my father-in-law was leading the seder, but I helpfully stickered his Haggadah with circled numbers keyed to a sheaf of supplemental materials on slavery. I got so carried away with annotating and supplementing, I thought, *Maybe I should just write my own Haggadah.*

This is not as arrogant as it sounds. New Haggadot are published all the time—it's not like I was signing up to write a new Bible. I'm not even a believer, and I own five different Haggadot, including one illustrated by Marc Chagall and one my big sister put together for her family's celebration.

So I set out to write one of my own. Habitual literature student that I was, I decided to begin with the primary source material: the Book of Exodus. Although I didn't believe the Exodus story was literally true, I planned to take from the original text and its language some powerful truths on the themes of slavery and freedom, tyranny and redemption.

Then I read it.

Passover, as originally conceived, celebrates neither freedom nor justice. It celebrates the triumph of one god over other gods, and one people over another. I was ready to accept the idea that throwing off the chains of oppression caused a certain amount of carnage and chaos. But the violence of Exodus is both intentional and impossible to justify.

Animals die first: countless fish from the water-turned-to-blood (Exodus 7:21), land animals from livestock disease (9:3), then anyone or anything caught in the worst hail and firestorm Egypt ever experienced (9:24–25). And then, for the tenth plague, brutality, not justice, is meted out:

> Every firstborn in the land of Egypt shall die, from the first-born of Pharaoh who sits on his throne to the firstborn of the female slave who is behind the handmill, and all the firstborn of the livestock. Then there will be a loud cry throughout the whole land of Egypt, such as has never been or will ever be again. (Exodus 11:5–7)

By the way, the reason it got to this gruesome point was that, as we all know, Pharaoh kept refusing to let the Hebrew people go. Except we all know wrong: Pharaoh *wanted* to let our people go, but every time he decides to, God hardens his heart (Exodus 4:21, 7:3, 9:12, 10:1, 10:20, 10:27, 14:4, 14:17). Plague by plague, the suspense ramps up and, with it, God's renown:

> I will harden Pharaoh's heart, and he will pursue them, so that I will gain glory for myself over Pharaoh and all his army; and the Egyptians shall know that I am the Lord. (Exodus 14:4; also 7:1–5, 9:16, and 11:9)

Sort of a pre-printing-press publicity stunt. Glory in the eyes of the Jews is an even greater obsession. We are to remember Him as "the Lord who took you out of Egypt" (Exodus 6:6,

10:2, 12:17, 12:27, 13:3, 13:8, 13:9, 13:14, 13:16, ad infinitum). We are in his debt and at his mercy:

> If you will listen carefully to the voice of the Lord your God, and do what is right in his sight, and give heed to his commandments and keep all his statutes, I will not bring upon you any of the diseases that I brought upon the Egyptians. (Exodus 15:26)

This isn't God the Father so much as *The Godfather*.

As for slavery, Exodus makes it clear: there's nothing wrong with *owning* slaves—just with *being* slaves. Now, I'm not a biblical scholar or a historian. The rules in Exodus 21 about how one is supposed to treat one's slaves may well represent, in the context of the biblical era, a giant moral leap forward. (Exodus 21:26: "When a slaveowner strikes the eye of a male or female slave, destroying it, the owner shall let the slave go, a free person, to compensate for the eye.") But Passover, as it is set forth in Exodus, is not an antislavery, anti-oppression holiday. It's an us-against-them, praise-the-Lord-or-suffer-the-consequences holiday.

I've never been to a seder that presents Passover as it is actually described in the Bible. Never. Some are more sectarian than others—more focused on the triumph of a chosen people—but all reach for general themes affirming that slavery is wrong and that the struggle against oppression is righteous. None include a prayer to the Almighty Enforcer (*Blessed art thou, Lord our God, Dispenser of Plagues, who has threatened us with disease and commanded us to follow His laws or else*) or a jaunty song about divine carnage (*Annnd . . . the first-born calf and the first-born slave and the first-born puppy too! God struck dead each one in turn but not a single Jew!*). The Jews I know, both believers and nonbelievers, comb through Exodus looking for phrases that meet our ethical standards, or they use Haggadot that do. The rest we leave out. We make scripture conform to our morality, not the other way around.

I remember once when I was a child standing next to my father during Yom Kippur services. We turned to such-and-such a page to read aloud a prayer about sin and repentance and, before I could begin, my father leaned over and whispered fiercely, "Don't you read that. It's not right: you're a child, you haven't sinned."

*It's not right.* Every day I imagine parents are leaning over and whispering some form of that message to their children. Or they are showing it by example. These parents don't get their morality *from* their scriptures—they bring their morality *to* it. Like the bar mitzvah boy who interprets his short portion of the Old Testament with extreme creativity. Or the priest who grants annulments with unorthodox leniency. Or the Presbyterian minister who performs same-sex marriage ceremonies, no matter what Romans 1:26–27 may say.

When it comes to scriptural morality, everybody picks and chooses. Some people focus on Jesus's teachings about compassion and humility and ignore what the Bible has to say about, say, homosexuality. But both moral edicts are in there: the good—"Let anyone among you who is without sin be the first to throw a stone at her" (John 8:7)—and the bad—"You shall not lie with a male as with a woman; it is an abomination" (Leviticus 18:22). Along with promoting the values of compassion, justice, and humility, the Bible extols the "values" of exclusion, patriarchy, tribalism, and, yes, homophobia. "To be a scriptural adept," writes Kwame Anthony Appiah, "is to know which passages to read into and which to read past."[12]

Some fundamentalist believers—the ones who tend to quote the bad parts approvingly and use them as justification for mistreating their fellow human beings—might think or at least want us to think that they have no choice in the matter: they are simply leaving moral questions up to God. But they are picking and choosing too. You can tell because while they might fixate on Leviticus 18:22, they seem less concerned about Leviticus 19:19 ("nor shall you put on a garment made of two different materials") or Deuteronomy 22:8 ("When you build a new house, you shall make a parapet for your roof").

Everybody picks among religious laws—even *religions* do. Bishops meet to decide if pro-choice politicians can take communion. Councils confer. Synods reinterpret. Religions changing their own rules over time is how same-sex couples can now get married in Episcopal churches and how women can be rabbis in some Jewish denominations. It's how some mosques are queer-inclusive and some have female imams. And it's how the Catholic Church was able to drop the concept of "limbo" from its catechism in 1992, after centuries of teaching that unbaptized babies ended up there, eternally caught between heaven and hell.

These doctrinal shifts are all signs of progress. But, again, they raise fundamental questions: Why do people dismiss some parts of their liturgy as passé and deem others to be relevant? Why do they use some parts of their tradition's message—"Love your enemies, do good to those who hate you" (Luke 6:27)—to invalidate another part—"Pursue your enemies, and attack them from the rear" (Joshua 10:19)? Why do progressive Muslims decide to ignore the injunction to "Slay the idolaters wherever you find them" (Quran 9:5) but uphold the directive to "feed the wretched poor" (Quran 22:28)? How do believers decide what's important in the Bible or the Quran and what should be ignored, downplayed, or dismissed as vestiges of another era?

*They pick the parts of the religious tradition that suit their values.* Which would mean their value system, by definition, is a separate entity from the religious tradition that it judges. A religious tradition can shape people's values. It can have a great deal of influence on how they think about the world—especially if they're convinced that it should supersede their own moral impulses. But still those impulses exist independently. If religion is moral, it's because people choose to make it so.

## GOD IS "JUST" JUST BECAUSE WE WANT HIM TO BE

THE SAME GOES FOR God. The idea that *God is good* is an extremely generous interpretation of texts that seem to argue otherwise. The Old Testament God—the Ten Plagues God—belongs to the fraternity of "psycho-gods," as social critic Barbara Ehrenreich calls them: "insatiable consumers of blood sacrifice, abettors of genocide, even, in the case of Zeus, a serial rapist."[13] Not only does God make Pharaoh harden his heart against the Jews *on purpose* so that he can continue to send plagues, he also tortures his own people as well, whether it's commanding Abraham to sacrifice his own son or allowing Satan to kill Job's children, destroy his property, and—why not?—cover him in boils.

If this were human behavior, we would not hesitate to call it immoral. And yet Jews as well as Christians are told, over and over, that God is good. Moses says, "His work is perfect, and all his ways are just. A faithful God, without deceit, just and upright is he" (Deuteronomy 32:4). Sure, I guess, if that's how you want to describe a guy who made escaped slaves wander in the desert for forty years before taking them to the promised land. And for the record, the brutality doesn't end on the last page of the Old Testament: even the supposedly kinder, gentler New Testament God promises to consign all unbelievers to everlasting hellfire.

Here on earth, we have no particular reason to believe God is good or just, but we have plenty of evidence that he is neither. I could fill a book describing the injustices that are occurring right now in this country alone, at this hour alone—injustices that, from a believer's perspective, God either causes or fails to prevent. These injustices pose a political problem for every moral person in America, of course, but they pose a terrible metaphysical problem for everyone who believes that God is just.

In 2012, for instance, a man killed twenty children, six adults, and himself in an elementary school in Newtown, Connecticut. Shortly thereafter, *New York Times* columnist Maureen Dowd asked Kevin O'Neil, a priest and family friend, to write about the tragedy from a religious perspective. This is from his essay, which bore the headline "Why, God?":

> How can we celebrate the love of a God become flesh when God doesn't seem to do the loving thing? If we believe, as we do, that God is all-powerful and all-knowing, why doesn't He use this knowledge and power for good in the face of the evils that touch our lives?[14]

It's tempting to answer this rhetorical question with *um, because He doesn't exist?* Seriously, reading this is like reading (in the paper of record, no less), "If we believe, as we do, that Santa knows who's naughty or nice, why didn't he bring any presents to that sweet child living in a shelter?"

Every once in a while, I am newly amazed by American culture's semi-official embrace of a fictional reality. O'Neil's queries gave me a strong urge to chuck the newspaper into my recycling. But I was too curious about the answer not to read on. I wanted to know: *Why, God?* What can believers say about the problem of an all-powerful God who permits (or causes) such horror? O'Neil's conclusion was essentially "I don't know" coupled with an assurance that God was present in the kindness we show one another in the face of tragedy. Where was God in that school on that day? "No matter what response I give, it will always fall short," he wrote. Indeed. As eighteenth-century Scottish philosopher David Hume said that our old friend Epicurus said:

> Is God willing to prevent evil, but not able?
> Then he is not omnipotent.
> Is he able, but not willing?
> Then he is malevolent.
> Is he both able and willing?
> Then whence cometh evil?

Is he neither able nor willing?

Then why call him God?[15]

"Whence cometh evil" is the question faced by everyone who believed in a good and powerful God and then heard about Newtown. O'Neil doesn't even attempt to explain how a just God, a good God, a moral God could cause (or permit) such a thing to occur. And how could he? The only God who has a motive for killing children is cruel or insane—a psycho-god. Which is, of course, possible. As humanist chaplain Greg Epstein has pointed out, given that God has never answered a prayer to regrow someone's limb, "There could be a god that hates amputees."[16]

Why not just accept the idea that God can be vengeful and cruel? It seems like that would be easier than trying to explain how a loving and just God lets children be murdered.

My guess is that, having their own innate sense of morality—believing that vengeance, brutality, cruelty, genocide, and baby-killing are wrong—believers want their God to agree with them. Believers don't want to believe in an unjust God. So they manage to think of God as the force they can call upon to help *after* "something awful happens,"[17] as Anne Lamott writes in *Help, Thanks, Wow*, but not as the force responsible for that awful thing. The alternative is that believers are left, time and again, with no way to explain why terrible events occur under the benevolent watch of a good and just God. It's an impossible assignment. All they can say is that he "works in mysterious ways" or variations thereof. "It was beyond our comprehension for those of us on earth to understand why," a church congregant told the *New York Times* after the 2022 massacre at Robb Elementary School in Uvalde, Texas. "It wasn't for me to understand why. God knows."[18] They don't have the clearance level or the intellectual capacity to understand. It's their limitation, not His failing.

But if God's behavior doesn't fit within the framework of human morality, if the behavior defies human understanding of right and wrong, then isn't human morality separate from God's morality? Aren't they two different things?

## THE TEN COMMANDMENTS

TO RECAP: HOLY BOOKS are rife with both moral and immoral passages, among which believers pick and choose because *they independently have beliefs about right and wrong*. God himself both commits and permits obscene injustices, which believers struggle to explain because *they independently know right from wrong*. So is there no connection at all between morality and religion?

What if we stripped religious precepts down to their purest form? Perhaps there are some core principles beneath the prejudices and factual errors, and perhaps those core principles could be a source of moral guidance. Perhaps they *are* a source of moral guidance whether we realize it or not.

Some people have told me that my children's horror at the infanticide in the Passover story, far from proving that one can be moral without religion, instead shows that religious morality is powerfully embedded in American culture. According to this argument, the Ten Commandments, the basic Judeo-Christian moral code, filtered its way down to my little atheists through *Blue's Clues* and *Charlotte's Web*, and through me—unwittingly—inflaming their indignation regarding the plight of the ancient Egyptian babies. When the stories age poorly and God disappoints, those stone tablets of wisdom still guide us. A North Dakota state senator, arguing for a law that would allow the Ten Commandments to be posted in classrooms, described the Decalogue as no less than "the foundation for moral living,"[19] and claimed that its absence from schools had led to a litany of social ills.

Unless the Supreme Court decides otherwise, North Dakota schools can now post the Ten Commandments along with "other" historical documents. I'm sure teachers across the state are relieved to have a time-tested tool for keeping kids on the straight and narrow.

TEACHER

Charlie, I saw you throw that. Please report to the principal immediately.

CHARLIE

It's not in the rules.

TEACHER

What?

CHARLIE

The rules. Right there. It says I have to honor my father and mother. Not you. Doesn't say anything about throwing pencils.

I submit that the Ten Commandments, as rules to live by, are pretty useless. The first four say nothing about how people should treat one another, only about how they should treat God. That leaves just six moral guidelines: (1) honor your parents, (2) don't murder, (3) don't commit adultery, (4) don't steal, (5) don't lie, and (6) don't envy. If we generously interpret "don't lie" to include don't deceive or mislead, and "don't steal" to include don't exploit or enslave (an interpretation that is not, as noted, endorsed by the Bible itself), we can perhaps keep students from cheating on tests and taking other students' lunch money. But can we keep them from sexually harassing a classmate or telling racist jokes or bullying someone on social media? Nope, not in there. Can we keep them from vandalizing the cafeteria or starting a fight in the locker room? Can we keep them from leaving a drunk friend alone at a party to get her own ride home? Sorry, no.

Now, you might argue that there's no way an ancient set of rules could anticipate revenge porn or doxing or securities fraud. I grant that cultural pertinence is not a fair test of true and abiding wisdom. To give the Ten Commandments a fighting chance, we would need to take the core reasoning behind each rule and apply that reasoning to our modern moment.

But the Ten Commandments don't explain much. They don't say *why* you shouldn't steal or murder or covet or lie, just that you shouldn't. Only a few of the Ten Commandments command significant tablet space. Don't worship idols (number two), for instance, gets a full backstory plus a specific threat of punishment.

> You shall not make for yourself an idol, whether in the form of anything that is in heaven above, or that is on the earth beneath, or that is in the water under the earth. You shall not bow down to them or worship them; for I the Lord your God am a jealous God, punishing children for the iniquity of parents, to the third and the fourth generation of those who reject me. (Exodus 20:4–5)

Now *that's* a commandment. Also, if you're wondering whether just you or you *and* your male and female slaves have to keep the sabbath, the fourth commandment does spell that out pretty clearly (Exodus 20:10). But murder, adultery, theft, and lying apparently require no further elucidation.

I guess that makes sense: the things we already know we're not supposed to do—*because we independently know right from wrong*—don't have to be explained. The wrongs that are not quite so obvious (that is to say, not quite so wrong)—like why not worship other gods too—must be insisted upon with dramatic rhetoric and bald threats.

Here again, my point is not so much that the Ten Commandments aren't useful; it's that their uselessness proves that people—even religious people—don't really use them to tell right from wrong.

It turns out the question we should ask isn't so much *where do atheists learn right from wrong?* It's *where does anyone?*

## IF NOT RELIGION, WHAT?

So WHERE DO WE get our notions of right and wrong? I believe it's simple—or at least it begins simply, with a recognition of our shared humanity. We register how it feels to be mistreated, assume other people would feel more or less the same way, and try not to mistreat them. It's a principle I invented completely on my own. I call it the "Rule of How Would *You* Feel?"™ It works for all sorts of basic ethical decision making, as well as for teaching children to consider their own ethical behavior, from bullying—"How would you feel if the cool kids decided to give you a nickname?"—to thank-you notes—"How would you feel if you went to the trouble to send a present and then you heard NOTHING?"

Hm, what's that? The Golden Rule?

Okay, fine. It's true that almost every religion and code of ethics you can think of has its version of the "Rule of How Would *You* Feel?" —the notion that "we must treat others as we wish others to treat us,"[20] as the Parliament of the World's Religions summarizes it, in "Towards a Global Ethic." According to that declaration, the rule is a "principle which is found and has persisted in many religious and ethical traditions of humankind for thousands of years." Jesus said, "In everything do to others as you would have them do to you" (Matthew 7:12). Muhammed said, "None of you has faith until he loves for his brother, or his neighbor, what he loves for himself."[21] Bahá'u'lláh said, "If thine eyes be turned towards justice, choose thou for thy neighbor that which thou choosest for thyself."[22] Jainism extends the principle to all creatures, not just humans: "A man should wander about treating all creatures as he himself would be treated."[23] Confucius said, "Do not impose on others what you yourself do not desire."[24] A Yoruba proverb counsels, "When one fells a tree in the forest one should apply the matter to oneself."[25]

I quote all these religious examples not to give the "Rule of How Would *You* Feel?" some ancient-wisdom heft so much as to demonstrate that this basic concept is so universal, so ingrained in the experience of being a human in the world, that it exists *outside* every religion and therefore has to be incorporated *into* every religion. But you don't need religion to live by it. It is a principle based not on the supernatural but on the human capacity to extrapolate from our own experience of the world to the experience of others.

It is also only a starting point. It works great for playground morality, interpersonal dilemmas, or quickly evaluating the words that are about to come out of your mouth. But as we get older and experience more of the world, our moral questions get more complex and more abstract. They demand more of us: they demand reason and research and second thoughts. Certain situations may turn "treat people the way you would want to be treated" into a real head-scratcher. You may wonder about the definition of "people": who precisely gets hurt if you sneak into a movie at the mall? You may have to balance competing goods or harms: is it okay to kill someone in self-defense? You may have to think about behavior long-term or more generally: is it okay to lie to someone if you think it will keep them safe? Modern life combined with a modern understanding of environmental consequences may force you to decide not so much whether to be good or bad as just how bad you are going to be. How much are you going to patronize global corporations that exploit labor? None? Less than your neighbor? As little as you can without inconvenience? Once you know that airplanes hasten climate change, are you still going to take that flight to visit your grown children? It's complicated.

And of course other people—from other cultures, in different circumstances—might not always feel the way you do about things.

But the "Rule of How Would *You* Feel?" is still a good place to start. Use yourself as a rough guide to how someone else would feel about bad things—being hurt, cheated, insulted, ignored, or embarrassed—and then try to keep others from feeling that way. Or try to help others feel how you feel about good things—being full, warm, heard, and safe.

Begin with your responsibility to respect the feelings and lives of other people, add in rationality, humility, and the willingness to investigate and to change course as a result of your investigation. And the rest is a matter of debate—both personally and politically.

The rest is the glorious, complicated puzzle of being a decent person.

## THERE'S ONE MORE PROBLEM

YOU DON'T HAVE TO believe in God to *know* right from wrong. But do you have to believe in God to *do* what is right? As Dmitri asks the skeptical seminary student Rakitin in *The Brothers Karamazov*, "If there's no God and no life beyond the grave, doesn't that mean that men will be allowed to do whatever they want?"[26] Let's say we used the "Rule of How Would *You* Feel?" to figure out the right thing to do. What makes us actually do it?

First, we need to dispense with the notion that believing in God makes *believers* do the right thing.

That might have been the original plan. In the fifth century BCE, a Greek playwright (maybe Critias, maybe Euripides—it's unclear) wrote a speech for the character Sisyphus, in which he posits that "some shrewd man" invented God to control men's behavior, even when no one could see them.

> So he thereupon introduced religion,
> Namely the idea that there is a deity flourishing with
> immortal life . . .
> Who will hear everything said among mortals,
> And will be able to see everything that is done.

If you plan some base act in silence,
The gods will not fail to notice.[27]

With the Greek gods, who liked to intervene in the lives of mortals, I imagine there was a notion that if they noticed bad behavior they would punish it. The fear of God's wrath seems to have continued into Old Testament days, when He went around smiting people, and rules like "Love your neighbor as yourself; I am the LORD" (Leviticus 19:18) carried an implied threat. Even today some people still think God is meting out punishments in the form of hurricanes and so forth.

But modern believers don't typically expect God to interfere in their lives—not in this life. Instead, the threat of eternal punishment supposedly acts as a deterrent: people refrain from doing wrong because they don't want to burn in hell for eternity. Hamlet would have killed himself if "the Everlasting had not fixed his canon 'gainst self-slaughter." The "future state of rewards and punishments" is, according to those discriminatory state constitutions, what keeps believers in line enough to be trustworthy public servants. Christian pastor Rick Warren sums up this idea in *The Purpose Driven Life*.

> If your time on earth were all there is to your life, I would suggest you start living it up immediately. You could forget about being good and ethical, and you wouldn't have to worry about any consequences of your actions.[28]

That's the general idea: no God = no divine punishment = no guardrails to human behavior.

But in reality, neither God himself nor the threat of divine retribution keeps religious people from doing bad things. No need to name names here. For evidence we can just go to the religions themselves. If the threat of eternal punishment were enough to keep believers in line, then there wouldn't be elaborate religious rituals of repentance and forgiveness, from Yom Kippur (the Jewish Day of Atonement) to Confession (the Catholic sacrament) to Salat al-Tawbah (the Muslim prayer of repentance) to Prāyaścitta (the Hindu concept of remorse and penance). If post-death punishment were a true deterrent, religious people would never need to have their slates wiped clean because they would never have dirtied them in the first place.

So, yes, Dmitri, *whether or not* there's a God and life beyond the grave, people are allowed to do whatever they want. Why aren't we all out living it up then, immorally and unethically?

Because "wants" don't have to be frivolous, felonious, immoral, or even selfish. When we refrain from stealing from the cash register or betraying a spouse, we may do so to avoid painful consequences: we want to keep the job and the marriage, stay out of jail, or avoid being judged, shunned, or despised. But we may also just want to be decent people. We may want to be liked and respected. We may want to be accepted in our community or want our community to be functional and peaceful. We understand all the benefits that accrue from being decent, and we feel a rush of pleasure (an actual, documented jolt of dopamine) when we do good.

Yes, we may be tempted to think only of our freedom and no one else's, or we may celebrate our personal triumphs and shut our eyes to the injustices of the world. And, yes, we may be tempted to ignore the dead babies if they're not *our* dead babies. But most people want to be worthy in the eyes of their children. We want to love, to be loved, and to deserve love. For atheists, and even for believers, it hardly matters whether God is good or wants us to be good. What matters is that we know what's bad—inside, we know—and we want to be good.

# TAKE ME TO CHURCH

*It is the world's great religions that have perhaps given
most thought to the role played by the environment in determining
identity and so—while seldom constructing places where
we might fall asleep—have shown the greatest sympathy
for our need for a home.*

ALAIN DE BOTTON, *The Architecture of Happiness*

THE ARCHITECTURE FIRM I write for had hired a Dutch company to redo our brand and website. At the project kick-off meeting, the team leader asked each of us to name our favorite place. "Kate, why don't you start us off?"

I was at my desk in my bedroom in Albany, facing my computer and the window beyond it—not so I could gaze upon the February-brown field but so my onscreen face would be lit, more or less, by the weak winter light. We were all in separate rooms: the Dutch quarantined by law during a Covid surge and the New Yorkers dispersed as a matter of convenience.

I panicked briefly. Should I try to impress these hip young Europeans or deflate their silly get-to-know-you game? Should I mention something famous or something obscure? But a place had popped into my head and would not be dislodged, so I decided to go ahead and name it: the Pazzi Chapel, Basilica di Santa Croce, Florence.

Why did I love it? They wanted to know. I looked away from the screen and saw myself sitting on a stone bench in the chapel. The vast and dazzling Santa Croce contains sixteen different chapels, countless works of art, and enough memorials to famous people to make you dizzy from hours of peering at floor, wall, guidebook, and back again. It's filled with a silvery light and what seems like the entire art and architectural history of the Renaissance.

But Santa Croce also offers escape: out of the central nave to the south, into the main cloister, with its perfect Brunelleschi arches, shaded stone walkways, and a trim green lawn. And from there, into the Cappella dei Pazzi, the Pazzi Chapel, which is as ornamentally restrained as Santa Croce is riotous. Its scale is still grand compared to normal life, but its domes, arches, and vaults feel within reach and, perhaps more important, within comprehension. Just a square topped by half a sphere. That's how it feels, anyway; that's the calm it conveys. White plaster walls alternate with the smooth, blue-gray sandstone called *pietra serena*—peaceful stone— to soothe the eye. There is stained glass, yes, and glazed terracotta tondos by Luca della Robbia, but mostly there is room to think. To rest on the stone benches built into the walls. To breathe.

❧

When I was a child sightseeing with my family in Europe, churches were the salvation of my tired little legs. Technically, churches were also the reason my legs were tired: my father was an architecture buff, and my parents were indefatigable sight-seekers, and, for a time, professional tour guides. A famous church, or even a significant church, or even a significant painting inside an insignificant church, was not to be missed. And so we trudged. But after dutifully examining the statue/triptych/stained glass window of art-historical import, and before moving on to the next entry in the *Blue Guide*, I was permitted a few moments to sit in a cool interior and stare admiringly at vaulted arches. I doubt I got architectural insight—I definitely didn't get religion—but I got rest and peace, and that was plenty.

I have loved churches ever since. Once released from parental supervision, I continued to include church resting as a regular part of my sightseeing habit. I have fed coins into a box to light up Giotto's frescos, admired St. Francis's vow of poverty, imagined the weight of Jesus's body in my arms as I contemplated Michelangelo's *Pietà*. I've been struck by the modest grandeur of the Synagogue in Florence and the petite perfection of Kahal Shalom on the Greek isle of Rhodes.

Even if you're not a sightseer or have never attended religious services, you've probably been in a house of worship for weddings, funerals, or rites of passage. Or for something not even remotely religious.

Here's an incomplete list of the things I have done in churches or synagogues: Attended nursery school. Shopped at a rummage sale. Gone contradancing. Heard choral concerts. Taken a child to a Mommy & Me class. Watched a child play Chopin at a Chopin competition and Prokofiev at a Russian music competition. Waited in the nursery area while a child had voice lessons. Voted. Gotten vaccinated. Accompanied a friend to an AA meeting. Cooked at a soup kitchen. Watched a child perform in *Into the Woods*. Taken a Pilates class. Toured a flower show.

In America, churches are unavoidable: they are ubiquitous quasi-civic buildings with social halls and meeting rooms that can be rented for events. I always enjoy my excursions into these places, and I like to read the bulletin boards and peek into the sanctuaries if I can. It makes me feel like I'm spying on America. It also gives me a small sense of loss. Here is something good that I can use but not possess.

What is that good thing exactly? What makes a church—or a synagogue or a mosque—an object of my desire?

## HOME AWAY FROM HOME

THE ONLY PLACE OF worship I ever officially belonged to was Beth El Congregation in Harrisonburg, Virginia. Everybody called it "Temple Beth El" or just "Temple," a nickname that for me evoked both the legendary temples of Jerusalem and golden-pillared Greek ruins like the Parthenon. Our Temple was less majestic: a mid-1960s building with a drop-ceilinged social hall and a shush-carpeted beige sanctuary freighted with modern Judaica.

Beth El was not particularly beautiful or grand, but it was mine. We belonged to it as members, but more important to me as a teen, it belonged to me. It was mine to invite guests to, mine to deride affectionately, mine to help clean after an event. I knew how to open the vinyl accordion partition that separated the sanctuary from the social hall. I knew what the water in the water fountain tasted like. I could be sent to the kitchen for paper napkins. And when my non-Jewish friends arrived for my bat mitzvah ceremony, I felt like I was the host, greeting them at the door, showing them where the bathrooms were. Beth El means house of God, but to me it wasn't so much the God part that mattered, it was the house part.

Many synagogues are called "Beth" something or other. The largest Reform synagogue in Albany is Beth Emeth (House of Truth), and my father-in-law's Orthodox synagogue is Beth Abraham-Jacob (House of, um, Biblical Patriarchs). The philosopher Alain de Botton describes synagogue as "a temple to house a book,"[1] because behind every synagogue altar is an ark, and inside every ark is a velvet-draped, bejeweled Torah scroll—a book inside a house inside a house. In *Real Good Church*, Rev. Molly Phinney Baskette describes how she breathed life back into First Church Somerville in Massachusetts, and she's very clear on the house part of the endeavor. She writes about pastoral care, community outreach, social justice, finances, and leadership, but Chapter One is called "The Building," and job one was the women's bathroom. (Job two: the nursery.)

An extra house: think about how that enlarges your world. An extra place where you feel safe. A place you can go if you need to pee. A place where you might find help if you need it, and where others might ask you for help if they need it.

I have been to a few get-togethers with a local atheist group. We meet at a coffeehouse or a brew pub or a diner near the section of highway we're about to clear of litter. We usually don't have a particular subject to discuss or event to plan; the point of our get-togethers is just to enjoy the company of like-minded people. Though I'm lucky enough not to need a safe group in which to be myself, I know I should help form that group for others. But I rarely do. I think that's partly because every Capital Region Atheists and Agnostics outing is an *outing*: you have to double-check the time and the place before you leave the house, then find the restaurant, then find your seat at the restaurant, and order and pay and generally suffer the discomforts of public gatherings. What might lure me out of the comforts of my home on cold nights after long days is another home. A house of (non)worship. Where I knew what to do with my coat and where the bathroom was and where they kept the coffee. A house that welcomed everyone—because everyone's a stranger there the first time—but conferred a special sense of belonging on those of us who chose to keep showing up. For this reason, I once seriously considered joining a synagogue in Albany. I didn't want spiritual guidance; I just wanted somewhere to rest.

My father tells the story of an emissary from a church down the road visiting my parents right after they moved to Broadway, Virginia. The lady said she wanted to welcome them to town and invite them to join the church. My parents replied that, er, actually, they planned to attend the synagogue in Harrisonburg. "That's just fine," she responded. "Just making sure you had a place to go."

"A place to go." That's why people continue to go to houses of worship even when they don't worship anymore. It's the house part they want. The sense of belonging and welcome and family—or, if family is too strong a word, familiarity.

## A TEMPLE OF BELIEF

PLACES MAKE US FEEL things. If your memories of 2020 and 2021 are faulty, your sense of chronology and events unreliable, the place-less-ness of the Covid-19 lockdowns could be why. Not being in physical places removed so much of what our brains use to remember things. We may have experienced plenty professionally and emotionally and intellectually, but if it all happened within the same space or on the same thirteen-inch laptop screen, does it feel like it really happened? It's like reading a digital book instead of a physical book: I love my Kindle, but I've noticed I remember much more vividly the physical books I read. The sensual experience—the feel, the weight, the color, the paper—makes an impression, and in that impression the ideas of the book can pool.

But places do more than make events memorable. I know this partly from working at an architecture firm but mostly from being a person. A badly designed hotel can make you feel confused, dumb, and trapped; a well-designed one can make you feel confident, smart, and free. Bad museum: overwhelmed, confused, bored. Good museum: curious, inspired, alive. In *The Architecture of Happiness*, Alain de Botton writes, "An ugly room can coagulate any loose suspicions as to the incompleteness of life, while a sun-lit one set with honey-coloured limestone tiles can lend support to whatever is most hopeful within us."[2] Our susceptibility to the built environment puts us at the mercy of architects and interior designers—"we are inconveniently vulnerable to the colour of our wallpaper"[3]—but it also means we can make spaces that make us feel certain ways and think certain things.

That's what, it seems to me, those gorgeous churches I visited as a child were trying to do.

> The very principle of religious architecture has its origins in the notion that where we are critically determines what we are able to believe in. To defenders of religious architecture, however convinced we are at an intellectual level of our commitments to a creed, we will remain reliably devoted to it only when it is continually affirmed by our buildings.[4]

Churches, synagogues, temples, and mosques all give their congregants a second home—that's crucial—but they also give them
wonder and awe. Just by paying their dues or showing up every
week, just by belonging, people get to own a small piece of a very big
thing, a small piece of grace and beauty and history and community. A sense that they are part of something larger than themselves,
something connected to the greater world or even to the eternal.
Imagine how that would feel to a tradesman or a peasant in Renaissance Florence, living in cramped and demoralizing quarters. The
Pazzi Chapel would be the opposite: it would be *moralizing*.

Leon Battista Alberti, fifteenth-century artist, author, math-
ematician, and architect (oh golly, I think we have to call him a
Renaissance man), in one of the first books of architecture ever,
*On the Art of Building in Ten Books* (1452), gives detailed and highly
opinionated instructions on how to build everything, including sacred buildings. In his writing, he conflates Greek and Roman temples with contemporary churches, and he lumps in the Greek gods
with the Catholic one (he refers to ancient times as "the primitive
days of our religion"[5]). So when he talks about how to build a temple, he's really talking about how to build, say, Santa Maria Novella
in Florence (he designed its upper façade).

What should a "temple" be, according to Alberti? He thinks
sacred architecture should embody dignity, as well as purity, sim-
plicity, and grace. Most of all, it must be impressive: not for the
gods, who are above such things, but for people, "who value them
so highly." Sacred architecture should be impressive enough to
remind people that the gods are of the highest importance and
therefore remind us to be reverent. "There is no doubt that a temple that delights the mind wonderfully, captivates it with grace and
admiration, will greatly encourage piety."[6]

A beautiful house of worship reinforces the idea of worship itself. It can be deeply persuasive. "Under the influence of the mar-
ble, the mosaics, the darkness and the incense," writes de Botton,
"it seemed entirely probable that Jesus was the son of God and

had walked across the Sea of Galilee."[7] In persuasive settings such as these, not just ideas but institutions and their representatives appear to merit trust. The Catholic Church is to blame for allowing priests to prey on children, but surely Catholic *churches*—the buildings themselves—buttressed the hierarchy and the institutional authority that made the faithful more susceptible. The higher the vaulted ceiling, perhaps, the lower our defenses.

I've fallen for this persuasive power myself, not as a defenseless child, but as a proud mom. When Jesse was thirteen, he was invited to audition for the Choir of Men and Boys at the Cathedral of All Saints, the seat of the Episcopal diocese of Albany. The fact that he would be singing religious music didn't bother us; he had already sung more than his share of Christmas carols and gospel songs. I didn't believe in the Messiah, but I believed in Handel's *Messiah*. I believed in Bach. Auditioning for the celebrated Cathedral Choir was a big deal, an impression intensified by the cathedral itself, which *looked* like a big deal: a nineteenth-century Gothic-revival cathedral complete with flying buttresses and a giant stained-glass rosette. It's the fifth-largest cathedral in America and can accommodate more than a thousand worshipers.

From an ivied side entrance, we pushed open a heavy wooden door with wrought-iron fixtures to enter the choir practice room. The audition was rigorous—scales, intervals, range check, sight-reading—and the music was as demanding, and the choirmaster was as exacting, as a young musical perfectionist could wish. Before we left, the director showed us the interior of the cathedral proper. It was vast and cool and dark but for the light streaming through the stained glass.

Driving home, besotted, I started to do the kind of calculations a parent does when her child wins a place on a travel soccer team and she is flattered into considering ridiculous logistics: *sure, the weekend obligation and the weekly practice would be tough, but I could bring my work with me or find a local coffee shop . . . I could make that my reading time! I could—*

Jesse interrupted my reverie. "Do they allow gay marriage?"

"Hmm?"

"I'm not doing it if they don't allow gay marriage."

When I got home, I looked it up; they didn't. They really, really didn't:

> Members of the Clergy Resident in or Licensed to Serve in this Diocese shall neither officiate at, nor facilitate, nor participate in any service, whether public or private, for the Celebration or Blessing of a Marriage or any other union except between one man and one woman.[8]

It turned out Albany was the only one of the five Episcopal dioceses in the state that didn't bless same-sex marriages, and the bishop of the diocese (Bishop Love, I kid you not) had a national reputation as a conservative who opposed the ordination of gay priests. I emailed the choirmaster and told him why Jesse declined to work for his organization, but when he called to assure me that the forces of progress were working on the problem from within, I wavered for a minute. Thank goodness my son was more principled—and more resistant to the persuasions of architecture—than I.

❧

Uncovering the ugly doctrinal underbelly of the Cathedral of All Saints was a good reminder that places of worship, by definition, include the worship part. The part that excludes me. While there are churches whose values I don't actively oppose, even churches whose values I positively admire, I can never truly give myself over to awe and wonder in a place whose reason for being is God. Before it's the home of any one person, a church is God's home. The foundations of even the most progressive, politically palatable church, synagogue, and mosque rest on God: God's authority, God's presence, God's very existence. None of which I credit. So while I can feel awe at the acts of human creation and cooperation that church architecture requires, while I can feel inspired by the play of light on stone, I cannot feel fully transported by a place of worship.

But I still want that feeling. And I am not alone: "In the absence of gods," writes de Botton in *Religion for Atheists*, "we still retain ethical beliefs which are in need of being solidified and celebrated."[9] We still need spaces that inspire us.

*Religion for Atheists* is a charming book that distills some things religion does well and proposes ways for the secular world to co-opt them. At the former, de Botton is a master; at the latter, he is a bit . . . impractical. Instead of temples to gods, he proposes temples to perspective and reflection. "A Temple to Perspective would hope to push us towards an awareness (always under threat in daily life) of the scale, age and complexity of the universe" and "A Temple to Reflection would lend structure and legitimacy to moments of solitude."[10] Sounds lovely. But he doesn't say who's going to build these temples; he just thinks them up and includes photorealistic renderings of them in his book.

De Botton himself notes that one of the things that religion does best is accumulate wealth. He writes, "Only religions have been able to turn the needs of the soul into large quantities of money."[11] Right. And therefore only religions can actually fund the construction of temples. De Botton devotes a whole chapter to how adeptly religions build institutions and extend brand identity. The problem is that without the institution, the authority it confers, and the money it can raise, it's unlikely that his delicious secular fantasies—of Agape Restaurants ("ideal restaurant of the future" where we break bread together with strangers) or of a university with a Department of Relationships and an Institute of Dying—could ever become commonplace.

Perhaps it is more useful to note that many Temples to Perspective and Reflection already exist. I'm thinking of monumental architecture on the National Mall or some of our great memorials to our fallen dead and civic heroes. There are scenic overlooks all around the country where, if you take a moment to pull over, you cannot help being awed by the view. There are towers you can climb and bridges you can cross that make you feel small, relatively speaking, but also enlarged by the artistic and engineering feats achieved by your fellow humans.

In other words, we already have Temples to Perspective and Reflection (and Progress and Sacrifice and Hope). But those are not quite church, since they offer awe and wonder without the creature comforts. You may be moved, but you probably don't know where to find the bathroom.

## HOME + TEMPLE – GOD = ?

SO WHERE CAN ATHEISTS access the binary power of church: the comfort of home and the inspiration of temple?

Some lucky few of us can gather as atheists in dedicated houses of nonworship, such as the Sunday Assembly (tagline: "Live Better. Help Often. Wonder More") at Conway Hall in London. The New York Society for Ethical Culture, housed in a fine old building on the corner of West Sixty-Fourth and Central Park West, offers a regular Sunday Platform. But as scarce and scattered as these God-free churches are, attending one would render me (and I imagine most atheists) a pilgrim rather than a parishioner.

A few institutions—noncommercial and nonreligious—have the wealth and power to build gorgeous buildings for daily use. Fancy colleges, for instance, pour money into their architecture and send calendars filled with campus glamour shots to their alumni in aeternum. If you walk around Yale or Stanford or Middlebury on a reasonably nice day, you might wind up not just impressed but moved. All this—for education. If you are lucky enough to enroll, you get, for a few short years, the golden ticket: home + temple. A place you belong and a place that makes you feel like you're a part of something important. In this case, what's important isn't God but learning. Susan Ackerman, a religion professor at Dartmouth College, says churches are "sacred centers" around which people organize their lives—and that Dartmouth's sacred center is Baker Library, with its clock tower, its majestic spire, and its Green-facing gravitas.[12] The Lawn at the center of the University of Virginia campus argues that the acquisition of knowledge is an absolute good—as does, I gather, the Middle Path through Kenyon College in Ohio. The Beinecke Library at Yale positively glows with the glory of the written word: How can anyone who studies there fail to absorb the sense of historic purpose involved in the act of *reading*?

I should note that one can—one should—question this magnificence, just as one should interrogate the glories of Santa Croce. What fortunate few do these exquisite libraries serve? From what crimes do these stained-glass windows distract? To what better purpose could these funds be put? But for me, those questions complicate rather than erase my sense of awe and longing.

For my birthday a few years ago, my parents bought me a membership to the Whitney Museum of American Art. This was not a practical present. I do not live in New York City. Since college, I have lived on a farm, fields on all sides; before college, I lived in an old farmhouse (fields on two sides) in a tiny Virginia town. But (therefore?) when that heavy plastic, highly designed card arrived in the mail, I cried: I had my golden ticket. And the next time we were in New York making our kids tire out their legs at art museums, I insisted we use the members' cloakroom. Here was what to do with my coat, and here was our bathroom—both of them housed in a beautiful paean to the value of art and abstraction. Home plus temple—mine!

Perhaps rare books and modern art aren't your thing. It could be a minor league baseball stadium, where you know which vendor makes the best burgers, you chuckle at the announcer's stale jokes, and you feel at peace when a hush falls over the crowd on fireworks night. It could be a one-hundred-degree yoga studio, smelling of eucalyptus oil and sweat, where your initial irritation at your space-hogging neighbor gives way, after an hour, to a kind of love. It could be a salsa club, where no one cares about your job, your politics, or your country of origin, as long as you can find the one (or the two) and move your hips. It could be a slightly tattered local movie theater where every interaction—with other patrons, with the young tattooed employees—is backlit with the shared understanding that you could be sitting in comfortable stadium seating at the metroplex, but you have chosen this place instead.

Harvard Divinity School students Casper ter Kuile and Angie Thurston published a study, "How We Gather," that identified different varieties of "church" for religiously unaffiliated millennials. These included an arts community in Washington, DC, called the Sanctuaries and Artisans Asylum, and a forty-thousand-square-foot makerspace in Allston, Massachusetts. "But the one that really threw me," ter Kuile later wrote, "was CrossFit. People didn't just talk about it as their community. 'CrossFit is my church' became the refrain."[13] Tara Isabella Burton writes in *Strange Rites* about how, at one point in her life, her church was the McKittrick Hotel, home of the immersive theatrical experience *Sleep No More*."[14]

Perhaps there is no single answer to the problem of church. Perhaps the answer is we each must find our own.

Or make them. My father is a Shakespeare professor and the co-founder of a theater company, but he does love architecture, and not just as a means to torture small children. I learned from him how to tell Norman from Gothic arches, and why, more or less, the Pazzi Chapel makes me feel the way it does. He has actually built his church: Blackfriars Playhouse—a reproduction of Shakespeare's indoor theater, in Staunton, Virginia. The ostensible point of the Blackfriars is to produce Shakespeare's plays in a place that mimics the original performance conditions (plus electricity), thus unlocking much of the genius of the plays. But that's not the only point. The Blackfriars is, simply, beautiful. A rich tableau of wooden beams and red cushions and golden light. People get married there. And because it's beautiful and also completely superfluous to the maintenance of human life, it says, *This is what we value.* Shakespeare is what we value. Theater is what we value. Its beauty confers value on everything that happens there, so when you are in the audience, it confers value on you. And when you return again and again, subscribe, donate, or volunteer, when you get to know the staff and the seating chart and the best bathroom to visit at intermission, that magical place becomes yours.

### THE MUSIC STUDIO

WHEN MY KIDS WERE growing up, there was a place I went at least two times a week, sometimes five. Its potholed parking lot made me shake my head, but it also made me smile because it told me I'd come home. Its hard wooden benches were comforting, though not comfortable; its scuffed halls were filled with familiar kids and grownups, some of whom had known my children since before my children could read. I could leave my kids for hours without informing anyone and without worrying a bit. (And I did once or twice, by accident, in the great game of after-school three-kid monte that Adam and I used to play.) We paid to belong; we grumbled about the policies; and we felt ourselves fortunate to have found the place, so fortunate that we even tried to get our friends to join. And all the members of that community were there because we shared a belief in the same higher power: not God, in this case, but music.

For more than fifteen years, my children's music school was my church.

It was housed in an old city school on an ugly stretch of a five-lane commercial artery between the suburbs and the city proper, with the car washes, nail salons, and gas stations. Though the building felt solid and permanent, it was not in itself inspiring. The ceilings were high, but the lighting was resolutely fluorescent; the wall-to-wall carpeting in the classrooms was an institutional blue-gray-green; the holiday decorations in each classroom were the same every year. You had to know the place was worth the potholes because you couldn't necessarily *see* that it was.

But, if you belonged to The Music Studio, you got awe and wonder too. Several times a year, we all dressed up and entered a pretty recital hall at the local university, with balconies, red velvet drapes, plush chairs, and a Steinway grand onstage instead of an altar. In front of the piano—just as at an altar—stood a big bouquet of flowers.

In the audience at that recital hall, my daughter first learned to suffer boredom quietly; a long Mass could not have done the job better. She doodled; she yawned; in her program, with my pencil, she assigned each performer a letter grade for fashion; she turned to me often to mouth the words, "This is so looonggg." And yet, when she had her first recital there—in an A+ outfit, naturally—she could not have been prouder or more solemn or more relieved afterward than if she had celebrated First Communion.

In that hall, my sons learned to act respectful and attentive and fidget discreetly (and make paper airplanes from their programs). At the end of every recital, no matter how they had played, they emerged into the large foyer for trays of sweets and plastic cups of lemonade, just like after services at church. And just as we would in a church social hall, we lingered longer than necessary over store-bought cookies, basking in the fellowship, hoping for a blessing from one of the teacher-deacons or maybe even a word of particu-lar praise from the pastor herself, the director of the school.

And as long as my kid wasn't the one playing, I could relax in one of those plush chairs in "my" balcony, staring up at the chandelier, transported by the strange and undeniable power of music. How could something be so useless and yet so essential? How could a teenager, playing something written by another teenager two hundred years ago, fill me with hope? These were things I could feel and think about all the time—in my car, in my kitchen—but I didn't. I thought about them there, in that beautiful room. Built by human beings—filled with human beings—reaching beyond their daily lives to touch something both universal and immortal.

ᴥ

Once you belong to The Music Studio, you always belong. That's what the director says. But the pandemic broke the physical connection—they took the benches out so no one could congregate to wait for their children—and my daughter's graduation will complete the schism. Though I will always feel connected to it, there will be a point when I will no longer feel it's my church.

Then what?

I'll just have to find another, despite the effort that might take. Even for many believers, church is not a given anymore, now that, as Rev. Baskette puts it, we're past "the age of civil religion, when everybody went to church because everybody else went to church."[15] That makes the job of revitalizing her church harder, but it also makes it more meaningful, since every week the people who come to her church are actively choosing to do so.

People for whom a place of worship is neither home nor temple (let alone both) won't choose to keep coming back. They'll show up for weddings and funerals and maybe a choir concert or an election. But if they don't believe in the existence of the deity in whose honor and service the place was built, they'll need another place where, as de Botton puts it, "the values outside of us encourage and enforce the aspirations within us."[16] I wish for each of us at least one place that performs this function, be it the local library or a neighborhood bar or the lecture hall at a nearby campus where visiting writers read. I wish for each of us a home + temple. If you don't have one, go find one. If you do have one, take a moment to see it, to recognize it anew, the next time you are fortunate enough to find yourself inside it.

# ARE YOU THERE, NOT ME? IT'S ME

*I cannot believe there is anybody who does not feel
a surge of anxious longing.*

WENDY BECKETT, *Sister Wendy on Prayer*

$\mathbf{I}$S PRAYING TO GOD when you don't believe in God a kind of
lying? It didn't feel that way when I was a kid. We didn't go to
synagogue very often as a family, but we did say prayers at home
before dinner on Friday nights, almost religiously, one might say.
We said three: for the candles, for the wine, and for the bread. The
candle one goes: "Blessed art thou, Lord our God, King of the
universe, who has sanctified us with thy commandments and commanded us to kindle the sabbath lights." I'm pretty sure none of us
literally meant that. I know I didn't. But I didn't mind saying it, in
part because we almost never said those words. We said, "Baruch
Atah Adonai, Eloheinu Melech haolam / Asher kid'shanu b'mitzvo-
tav v'zivanu l'hadlik ner shel Shabbat." See? Completely different.

When we went to synagogue on the sabbath, the service we
heard was composed almost entirely of prayers in effusive praise of
God. Not prayers of supplication—the sabbath is a day of rest for
Jews and for God, so we don't *ask* for things. We just admire. The
blessing after a reading from the Haftarah (a collection of passages
from the Old Testament prophets) is fairly representative. It begins
thus: "Blessed is the Lord our God, Ruler of the universe, Rock
of all creation, Righteous One of all generations, the faithful God
whose word is deed, whose every command is just and true."[1]

I said that prayer when I was bat mitzvah, but I've never said it in English—looking it up for you here might be the first time I've even *read* it in English. Instead, I recited a pleasantly foreign aggregation of syllables that I had carefully learned by heart.

That's probably why praying didn't feel like lying, even though my mouth was saying things my head rejected. Sometimes we *did* say our Shabbat prayers in English, helpfully translating for non-Jewish dinner guests, but in that case we always put the words in what you might call *prayer quotes*: We pronounced "blessed" with two syllables and used outdated English like "art thou" and "thy." This was not everyday language that we would use, say, to praise our mom for making us dinner once again. It was not our vernacular. And since they clearly weren't *my* words, it was easy to let them slip from my mouth without first testing them for accuracy. It was like saying, "O, that this too, too solid flesh would melt, thaw, and resolve itself into a dew" without ever having personally entertained a suicidal thought.

Praying in a foreign language can separate spoken words from their felt meaning. That's one of the reasons that, in 1962, the Second Vatican Council of the Roman Catholic Church voted to recommend that much of the Mass be celebrated in the everyday language of a church's locale—the vernacular—rather than in Latin. "In order that the liturgy may be able to produce its full effects" on the faithful, "their minds should be attuned to their voices." Pastors of souls should ensure that their congregants "take part fully aware of what they are doing."[2]

Another reason the Catholic Church switched to the vernacular was more practical: they wanted to attract and retain priests, but fewer and fewer potential candidates knew Latin. Possibly the switch helped. But I bet the translation to the vernacular also dissuaded some potential priests—and drove off some congregants too. A language you don't know retains a sense of mystery and grandeur and, perhaps crucially, resists both comprehension and intellectual commitment. A language you don't know allows you more easily to say things you may not mean.

Sticking with Hebrew is how, if I'm visiting my parents on a Friday night and someone thinks to pause before dinner to light the candles, I still praise God, his commandments, the wine, and the bread.

## MAKING MANY INTO ONE

MOST OF THE PUBLIC prayers I heard growing up in a mostly Christian Virginia town were, by contrast, only too comprehensible. Each one would start out ecumenically enough in a "We are gathered here today" sort of way. But then the prayer would start to wind down and I would reflexively hold my breath: Was Jesus about to be invoked or wasn't he? Very likely he was.

On the rare occasion that he wasn't, I settled into the subsequent PTA meeting, graduation ceremony, awards dinner (or what have you) with a pleasant, surprised, warm feeling that maybe I *did* belong after all. Maybe my non-Christian existence had been recognized. Maybe the inspiring thoughts I just heard applied to me too.

More often than not, though, by the end of the prayer, we were all welcomed together or invited to do our best "in the name of our Lord and Savior Jesus Christ." Well, that let me out! Sure, it was a technicality—whether Jesus was my lord and savior was obviously irrelevant to the question of whether I was united in purpose with my fellow American Legion essay contestants—but it doesn't take much to go from insider to outsider. The sense of belonging is a fragile thing.

All I wanted in those moments was nonsectarian prayer. Twenty years later, two residents of Greece, New York, wanted the same thing. Plaintiffs in *Town of Greece v. Galloway*, they filed suit in 2008 against their small town, "alleging that the town violated the First Amendment's Establishment Clause by preferring Christians over other prayer givers and by sponsoring sectarian prayers. The plaintiffs sought to limit the town to 'inclusive and ecumenical' prayers that referred only to a 'generic God.'"[3]

Inclusive and ecumenical. Was that too much to ask? As a kid, I didn't question the notion that religious belief was the default, something we each shared in our own way. I just thought public prayer should leave room for all religions. A generic God would be just fine. That's the basic idea expressed by the opinion in another prayer-at-town-meeting case, *Joyner v. Forsyth County*: "those of different creeds are in the end kindred spirits, united by a respect paid higher providence and by a belief in the importance of religious faith."[4] In that 2011 case, the Fourth Circuit Court agreed with the plaintiffs, ruling that only nonsectarian prayer should be allowed. But in *Greece v. Galloway*, the Supreme Court held that a town wasn't violating the Establishment Clause even if the prayers that started its meetings were sectarian. Even if they were "we acknowledge the saving sacrifice of Jesus Christ on the cross"–level sectarian.

In his decision, Justice Anthony Kennedy explained that it was completely fine that 116 out of 120 invocations in the past dozen years had been explicitly Christian, as long as the town had clearly stipulated that all faiths were welcome to give the invocation. He took pains to point out, too, that the prayer is delivered "during the ceremonial portion of the town's meeting," when no actual policy is being made. You can even get there late, skip that part, and still get your business done.

But why have prayers at all if they don't matter?

Ah, but they do. Kennedy himself says that prayers "solemnize the occasion" and "unite lawmakers in their common effort." The part of the meeting he dismisses as "ceremonial" is, in his own words, "a moment for town leaders to recognize the achievements of their constituents and the aspects of community life that are worth celebrating."

In *Joyner v. Forsyth County*, Judge J. Harvie Wilkinson wrote that invocations at the start of legislative sessions

encourage participants to act on their noblest instincts; and
foster the humility that recognition of a higher hand in human
affairs can bring . . . it can bring together citizens of all backgrounds and encourage them to participate in the workings of
their government.[5]

You see, "ceremonial" is not merely decorative. It *means* something. No—it *does* something. Ceremonial prayers can harness
the collective mood; they can point the way forward. Great civic
prayers imbue people with a sense of purpose and inspire in them
a desire to be their best public selves.

But they can't do that work for nonbelievers, not if they speak of
God, even the vague "generic" God that the plaintiffs in both cases
sought. Which means that both the cases I have cited here—the
one that went "right" and ruled against sectarian prayer and the
one that went "wrong" and ruled for it—argue for a kind of civic
prayer that excludes me.

As a Jewish child in a Christian town, I didn't look at it that way.
But as an atheist adult in a largely religious country, I do. Inclusive
and ecumenical wasn't too much to ask. It was too little.

Kennedy knew atheists existed. He wrote, "Should nonbelievers
choose to exit the room during a prayer they find distasteful, their
absence will not stand out as disrespectful or even noteworthy."[6]
Uh, sure. But even if it were true that, as he asserts, we wouldn't be
penalized for skipping the prayer, wouldn't we be missing something? If prayer does what he says it does, isn't skipping the prayer
*itself* a penalty?

What if I want to solemnize the occasion of my appearance before
the board? What if I need my noblest instincts to be encouraged?

There is a way. Instead of leaving *me* out, public prayers could
leave out God. One can write prayers—ceremonial expressions
of communal intention, aspiration, and gratitude—without reference to a supernatural being or even to a vague, godlike "higher
providence."

If you'd like to hear a public prayer that doesn't feature God, I recommend the poem that Amanda Gorman wrote for the 2021 inauguration of President Biden. "The Hill We Climb" acknowledges the "never-ending shade" that surrounds us and urges us to keep moving forward and face the work we have yet to do as Americans.

> When day comes, we step out of the shade
> Aflame and unafraid
> The new dawn blooms as we free it
> For there is always light
> If only we're brave enough to see it
> If only we're brave enough to be it.[7]

That kind of verbal flourish is a bright yellow coat not suitable for all drab parka functions. But we could come up with something for the more mundane occasion of, say, a planning board meeting on the fourth Tuesday of every month. Where a dozen citizens have traded the comfort of their couches for Town Hall's folding chairs. Where a dozen citizens have taken the time to speak or listen under cold fluorescent lights. We can create ceremonial language that does justice to each of them, no matter what their beliefs about God.

It could start simply, so no one gets too embarrassed. Maybe the town clerk or the chair of the planning board would stand.

> Good evening, and welcome to the [date] meeting of [name of governing body]. We gather as citizens and stewards of [name of municipality] to work together on behalf of this [town, city, etc],

Enter a bit of ceremony:

> to honor its past, improve its present, and prepare for its future.

Finally, the prayer:

> May a spirit of cooperation guide our discourse tonight, and
> may our efforts be ennobled by wisdom and courage.

Guess what two-syllable word signifies fervent assent but not necessarily religious belief?

Amen.

## CHANNELING OUR EMOTIONS

THOSE CEREMONIAL WORDS ARE . . . fine. They're not perfect.
But prayer is about something other than, and something more
than, perfect words. Gorman's inaugural poem was a magnificent
moment, but a critic could argue that stepping out of the shade
and being in/being the light aren't super fresh or subtle images.
I would venture that "The Hill We Climb" was a better prayer
than a poem, that Gorman's words were something *better* than perfect. They were just loose enough to hold our trembling sense of
hope, and just firm enough to channel it toward determination.
Christian thinker C. S. Lewis wrote in *Letters to Malcolm: Chiefly
on Prayer* that the words of a prayer "serve to canalise the worship
or penitence or petition which might without them—such are our
minds—spread into wide and shallow puddles."[8]

We needed Lewis's canal that day—a channel everyone could
use—and Gorman built us a lovely one. Her prayer was made of
more than just words. It was also made of a cold day and the Cap-
itol steps, a yellow coat and a red hairband, a strong voice and a
young, glowing face. It was made of those listening who were united in relief at Donald Trump's removal and in disbelief at his ever
having been president.

People need that sense of connection, that feeling of being channeled from separate units into fleeting, precious community by an able leader. Prayers without God in them can give us that. But on the off chance that your local school board does not implement such a practice, you can still find moments of prayerlike communion, moments when you are led into sync with perfect strangers. Sometimes they have words. Sometimes they don't.

At a concert, perhaps. You arrive as an individual, a separate being, find your seat, arrange your coat, wish the person in front of you weren't so tall. The show begins and you become a collective noun, an audience. If you're lucky, sometime during the performance, the performer finds a way to turn you and your fellow audience members, the plural *you*, into a community, a congregation, a fleeting *one*.

I've seen Josh Ritter do that in concert. And maybe you've seen your favorite singer-songwriter (or pop star or rock group or rapper) do it too. He's singing "Kathleen," a light but perfect song in which the "I" offers to give a girl a ride home from a party. A verse in, we notice Ritter noticing that the audience knows the words; they're all singing along. When he gets to the bridge, he stops singing and lets the crowd do it, his arms outstretched, half conducting them, half gesturing in obeisance, his face beatific with joy.

> I'll have you back by break of day
> I'm going your way anyway
> And if you'd like to come along
> I'll be yours for a song.

These words are not complicated—they're a perfect nothing, a trifle—but the moment feels like nothing less than a congregation united in prayer. In *Good without God*, Greg Epstein suggests that the secular alternative to prayers might be great songs. Maybe greatness helps, but I don't think it's essential. The song is just a channel. The beauty and architecture of the channel itself might inspire awe. But any sturdy, empty vessel will do. Like religious prayer, its effect depends greatly on circumstance. A brilliant sing-er-songwriter in concert with his fans, yes. A hometown crowd at Camden Yards, singing "Thank God I'm a Country Boy" in the middle of the city of Baltimore? Yes to that too.

I've even seen it happen *silently* in a set by the comedian Pete Holmes. When he's making a point about the marvels of human consciousness, he asks the audience to sing "Happy Birthday" silently. "Everybody—we'll all do it—everybody sing 'Happy Birthday' in your heads right now." When we're done, he asks, in wonder and not really for a laugh, "How are you hearing that?" "Happy Birthday" is pretty banal, the lowest common denom-inator of tunes. But that's the point: we all know how it goes. Holmes picks a universal tune so that everyone in that audience can access the transcendent experience of thinking the same song in unison with strangers, of marveling together that we have ears, as Holmes puts it, both outside and inside our heads, that our brains are pieces of meat that can remember a tune, and even play it, in silence.[9]

And then play it again, as he instructs us: still silently, but *louder*.


## CONVERSATIONS WITH GOD

WHEN WE DID ATTEND Shabbat services in my childhood, I enjoyed praying aloud, in Hebrew and sometimes in prayer-quot-ed English. There weren't many moments of oneness, but it was a comfortable feeling of community. It felt good to be with others, to speak along with others, to fill a communal space with sound.

But sometimes the rabbi asked us to stand and pray silently, and I was hopeless at that. Maybe I spent the first nine seconds con-templating the topic of the day, but then my thoughts spilled into a wide and shallow puddle, or simply evaporated. I watched the sports jacket in front of me shift its weight under the burden of standing. I itched to gather the lock of hair that had escaped the taut ponytail ahead to my left. I longed for the relief of sitting in the pew again even as I had, only minutes before, longed for the relief of standing up from it.

I understand now one reason those moments were so excruciating: I didn't believe that anyone was listening to me pray. Definitely not some deific bush that was burning to hear about my day or poised to smite my middle-school nemesis. And not a kindly father commiserating or a universe attending either. "What is more natural and easier, if you believe in God, than to address Him?"[10] asks C. S. Lewis. What is more unnatural and difficult if you don't?

In *Learning to Pray*, James Martin, a Jesuit priest, defines prayer as a "conscious conversation with God."[11] Whether that's a heart-to-heart with "our ultimate best friend," as Catholic writer Mary DeTurris Poust describes God,[12] or whether "reverence and awe are in order,"[13] as Martin would have it, we're talking to *someone*. Anne Lamott explains in *Help, Thanks, Wow*, "Prayer means that, in some unique way, we believe we're invited into a relationship with someone who hears us when we speak in silence."[14]

Private prayer would therefore seem like an obvious time for atheists to bow out. After all, our defining characteristic is believing that there is no "someone" out there to hear us. We can have public prayer, since it depends not on God so much as on words, feelings, moments, and, most important, other human beings. But private prayer? What could an atheist get from that? And how would we even do it?

Some writers on prayer strongly imply that atheists already do pray; we just don't call it that. Wendy Beckett asks in *Sister Wendy on Prayer*: "Has everybody not experienced a moment when beauty or wonder touched them at depth?"[15] Martin has a whole chapter called "Praying without Knowing It." "Even if you're an agnostic or an atheist," he says, "you've probably had some of these experiences."[16] These include "You pause to think about something that inspires you," "You're aware that you feel compassion," "You wonder about the meaning of your life."[17] Beckett's experience of art (she's an art historian) fits right in there: "I have only to see a Cézanne, for example, perhaps one of his great landscapes, . . . and I am overwhelmed with joy."[18]

Martin describes a moment in his childhood—before he became truly religious—when he stopped in the middle of a bike ride to look at the surrounding meadow: "All around me was so much life—the sights, the sounds, the smells—and suddenly I had a visceral urge not only to be a part of it, but also to know it and somehow possess it. I felt loved, held, understood."[19]

To me, these sound like moments of transcendence; they are moments that happen to you, moments when you are struck with the largeness of life. Prayer, on the other hand, is something that you set out to do with purpose.

Here is where we hit a snag. What would be the purpose of atheists praying?

Well, what is the purpose of prayer for people who *do* believe? It can't be getting things they ask for, since the prayers of believers aren't answered any more than ours would be. I know this is obvious, but it's worth saying, not because it means that prayer is silly, but because it means that believers must get something from praying other than the things they ask for when they pray.

To be fair, the Bible does strongly imply that God answers specific prayers. Mark says Jesus said, "So I tell you, whatever you ask for in prayer, believe that you have received it, and it will be yours" (Mark 11:24). The Quran too: "And your Lord has said, 'Call upon Me, and I shall respond to you" (Quran 40:60). But most people who've begged God to intercede in their lives realize that he doesn't exactly do so. Mark Twain illustrates this realization in *Huckleberry Finn*, in which Miss Watson tells Huck to pray and "whatever I asked for I would get it." Huck soon discovers, as he tells the reader,

> it warn't so. I tried it. Once I got a fish-line, but no hooks. It warn't any good to me without hooks. I tried for the hooks

three or four times, but somehow I couldn't make it work . . .
I set down, one time, back in the woods, and had a long think
about it. I says to myself, if a body can get anything they pray
for, why don't Deacon Winn get back the money he lost on
pork? Why can't the widow get back her silver snuffbox that
was stole? Why can't Miss Watson fat up? No, says I to myself,
there ain't nothing in it.[20]

Mark Twain was famously a skeptic; he *would* say "it warn't so."
But Christian thinker and writer C. S. Lewis says essentially the
same thing: God doesn't answer prayers.

Every war, every famine or plague, almost every death-bed, is
the monument to a petition that was not granted. At this very
moment thousands of people in this one island are facing as
a *fait accompli* the very thing against which they have prayed
night and day, pouring out their whole soul in prayer, and, as
they thought, with faith.[21]

Lewis even admits that it would be easier if Christianity gave up
the notion of petitionary prayer, as it forces Christians to attempt
to explain the contrast between "Whatever you ask for in prayer
with faith, you shall receive (Matthew 21:22) and *what actually happens in their lives.* Twain is not the only humorist to laugh about
it. "When I was a little boy," goes a bit by comedian Emo Philips,
"I used to pray every night for a new bicycle. Then I realized the
Lord in his wisdom doesn't work that way. I just stole one and
asked him to forgive me."[22]

Martin excuses God's apparent inattention with the traditional
"mysterious ways" shrug: "Why some prayers seem answered in
ways that we would like and others are not is beyond our powers
of comprehension."[23] Beckett says, "The essential nature of our
plea is not that God will change the real world, but that he will
strengthen us to bear the impact of it."[24] Lewis pins the failure on

the faithful: "We must conclude that such promises about prayer with faith refer to a degree or kind of faith which most believers never experience."[25]

Howsoever they manage to explain the gap between promise and delivery, these writers all concede—as all writers of faith who are attempting to write in good faith must concede—that God won't necessarily answer prayers per se. But they pray anyway.

Why?

I imagine it would be a comfort to believe that someone is listening—someone whose feelings you can't hurt, whose time you can't waste, whose sensibilities you can't shock. I imagine that might be especially the case in a crisis—under the harsh lights of a hospital room when your whole self is focused on a single, desperate hope. (People may scoff that God is an "invisible friend," but that sounds pretty nice to me.) Atheists can't believe someone is listening. But it turns out that acting *as if* someone is listening could work just as well.

According to a study detailed in the *Journal of Experimental Social Psychology*, communicating with a deity you know to be imaginary can be empowering.

> Participants who were asked to pray about a topic of their choosing for five minutes showed significantly better performance [on cognitive tasks] compared to participants who were simply asked to think about a topic of their choosing. And this effect held regardless of whether participants identified as religious (70 percent) or not.[26]

Why does this work? Apparently, even nonbelievers interpret prayer as a social interaction with God—a conversation, as in Martin's definition. And *social interactions* increase cognitive function. Just putting themselves in the praying frame of mind rather than the thinking frame of mind gave these participants strength to face the mental tasks the study had set for them.

It may seem odd to do this intentionally, and not for the purposes of a science experiment, to play both parts in a prayer: you and God. But if you think about it, of course, believers do this too.

Martin inadvertently makes this apparent in the chapter "How Do I Know It's God?" He posits a "you" trying to pray. You "hear" some thought or emotion or answer and you wonder whether that's "you" or "God." The answer, says Martin, is if the voice seems godly—if it's encouraging you toward good things and not bad or frivolous things—then it's God. "A simple way to understand it is that if you are feeling despair, hopelessness, or uselessness, this is not coming from God."[27] "When you feel despair, don't listen to it; when you feel hope, follow it."[28] A sense of calm? That's God. A sudden thought that you need to check your email? That's you.

"God," in other words, is all your good and positive impulses grouped together and given a name. It's you, but separate. "Let's not get bogged down on whom or what we pray to," Lamott says. "We could call this force Not Me."[29] Okay. So to divide me from Not Me—to divide mundane, needy, distractable me from calm, wise, compassionate Not Me—we're going to have to do a bit of mental mitosis.

We can manage that. We can sing "Happy Birthday" without making a sound. We can listen in Spanish and respond in English. We can look at a bunch of squiggles on paper and know how to bake a cake, or we can look at a different bunch of squiggles and know how to play a tune. Double the recipe? Transpose the key? Read the next sentence in an Australian accent? No worries, mate.

I've seen the comedian Hannah Gadsby plant a punchline at the beginning of a long and funny story and time it precisely to go off *in the minds of the audience members* at the end of the show. She never said it. She just made two thousand people think it.

Heck, to satisfy our desire for causality and calm our fear of mortality, we can invent a benign and invisible supernatural being who promises both divine justice and life after death.

If we can do all that, I think we can manage to sit on both sides of a prayer. We can be speaker and listener, penitent and confessor. Some Christian prayer guides suggest as much. Lamott may say we're praying to Not Me, but she also says, when she prays the Serenity Prayer to God, "I am at the same time alerting the person inside me that I need to rein myself." She calls prayer a "memo to self."[30]

## AN EXERCISE IN TRUTH-TELLING

WE CAN BE BOTH the writer and the reader of that memo. But what could we tell ourselves that we don't already know? The same could be said of God, of course. "To confess our sins before God is certainly to tell him what He knows much better than we,"[31] says Lewis. The point, for him, is the act of telling. "The change is in us. The passive changes to the active. Instead of merely being known, we show, we tell, we offer ourselves to view."[32]

We offer ourselves to view. Beckett says, "One of the effects of prayer is that it exposes us to ourselves" (there we are again, doubled or split). "If we pray, that comfortable cloak that assures us of our virtue begins to fray, to dissipate, to uncover the sorry nakedness of what we really are."[33]

Truth is what we're after here, a level of honesty about ourselves and with ourselves that's difficult to achieve in our daily lives. "It is no use to ask God with factitious earnestness for A when our whole mind is in reality filled with desire for B," writes Lewis. "We must lay before him"—lay before ourselves, that is—"what is in us, not what ought to be in us."[34]

This is the crux of one of the great soliloquys in *Hamlet*, when Claudius tries to pray. He doesn't know how because he understands that, unlike in his regular life, he won't be able to buy his way out of the truth.

In the corrupted currents of this world
Offence's gilded hand may shove by justice,
And oft 'tis seen the wicked prize itself
Buys out the law: but 'tis not so above;
There is no shuffling, there the action lies
In his true nature; and we ourselves compell'd,
Even to the teeth and forehead of our faults,
To give in evidence.[35]

In the end, he can't do it: "My words fly up, my thoughts remain below."[36] Prayer, says Beckett, "is the only human activity that depends totally and solely on its intrinsic truth."[37] I can lie in Hebrew and get pleasure and a sense of occasion out of it. I can sing (or imagine) a song filled with lines I don't believe in and feel a flush of human connection. But what if I am saying something to Not Me? Without truth it would be truly worthless.

To pray is to look for truth within ourselves and reveal it to ourselves. True desire. True hope. True gratitude. True need. True intention.

## WHERE TO BEGIN?

ANDREW W. K. ONCE wrote in his *Village Voice* advice column a useful guide to praying without God. He was responding to the question, "Prayer Is Stupid, Right?" from someone whose brother was dying. He said,

Just focus on every moment you've ever had with your brother. Reflect on every memory, from years ago, and even from just earlier today. Let the feelings wash over you. Let the feelings take you away from yourself. Let them bring you closer to him. Let yourself be overwhelmed by the unyielding and uncompromising emotion of him until you lose yourself in it.[38]

Maybe atheists can't pray "for" people, as believers do, asking God to relieve their suffering, but we can pray *about* people, asking our minds to relive our time with them, feel thankful for them, swim in our love and worry for them. It won't help them get better, but it will help us be more connected in their presence. It will help us feel what we need to feel in the moment.

This is prayer in a crisis, prayer that channels grief and despair in an effort to keep them from overflowing the banks of sanity. It's the kind of prayer I hope not to need often. But there's another kind of prayer, the prayer of daily practice, a channel to use every day. For that, Martin suggests—yes, for Christians, but we can use it too—the Ignatian Examen. St. Ignatius of Loyola, a sixteenth-century Spaniard who founded the Jesuit order, wrote a series of *Spiritual Exercises* that includes the "examination of conscience," to be performed daily.

There are five sequential parts: Presence, Gratitude, Review, Sorrow, and Grace. "Presence" is allowing yourself to feel that you are in God's presence or, let's say, in the presence of Not You. Tune yourself to that praying channel. Then follows "Gratitude," which we need no God to receive, only a self to feel. Then "Review" your day in sequence if you can, as honestly as you can. Feel "Sorrow" for what you regret, where you went wrong, whom you harmed. And give yourself the "Grace" to do better tomorrow.

I tried this and have so far failed. The first problem is that there's no structure for prayer in my life. I do not hear the adhan, the Muslim call to prayer, five times a day; I do not rise every morning to wrap tefillin, small Jewish prayer boxes with straps, around my arms and hands; and I do not kneel every week or more at Mass. Without religion there is no "thing you are obliged to do regularly, at an appointed time, to remind you of your values even when you are grouchy, busy, or annoyed,"[39] as Sasha Sagan puts it. No external authority telling me I must. Just me and Not Me, if I can find her.

Many days I walk up and down my driveway—one return trip is one mile, about twenty minutes at a thinking pace. Perfect for an Examen. The first time I tried it, I got to step one—being present with Not Me—and then my mind wandered and I pulled it back. The gratitude part was easy, but the review was impossible as I raced ahead of the day's events to circle my worries. I thought about what changes I could make to move forward with grace, but the next day I forgot them.

Lewis says of prayer, "We are reluctant to begin. We are delighted to finish."[40]

Reminding myself I was just a beginner, I tried a junior version of the Examen, a team-building exercise Lena learned in high school called Rose, Thorn, and Bud. You share one good thing that happened to you that day, one bad thing, and one hope or possibility or thing you're looking forward to. We've used this to catch up on each other's days, especially during the pandemic when we needed to remind ourselves that each day was different from the last. On my own it was harder: do I pick a rose that I felt in the moment or a rose I only spot looking back? "Thorn" sounds so mild. Could I add aphids and drought to the metaphorical mix? Or is the *point* of the exercise to minimize one's troubles? I scolded myself and started over.

Lewis says, "The fact that prayers are constantly set as penances tells its own tale."

Oh how the mind wants to jump its channel! Oh how I want to tell Not Me a tidy story in which the harm I have caused today can be remedied tomorrow! Oh how I would rather leave the whole blessed mess unexamined! Oh—a hawk!

Lewis says, "Prayer is irksome. An excuse to omit it is never unwelcome."

Atheists have a great excuse to omit prayer, just as we have a great excuse—in the words of a Freedom From Religion Foundation publicity campaign—to sleep in on Sunday. Who would even expect prayer of us? But I am not an atheist because I want to get out of stuff. I'm not the sort of person who takes the easy way. I am (or I want to be) the sort of person who is willing to do difficult things if they can bring her closer to living life fully, thoughtfully, and joyfully. And—hardest of all—honestly. So if prayer is a channel I can travel to arrive at truth, to make myself think more honestly about myself and the world around me, then I want to try it. Even if I'm bound to fail more days than not, even if I have to practice, and even if it is sometimes impossible not to think about dinner.

# RITE OF PASSAGE

*And there are always new thresholds to cross: the thresholds of
summer and winter, of a season or a year, of a month or a night;
the thresholds of birth, adolescence, maturity, and old age . . .*

ARNOLD VAN GENNEP, *The Rites of Passage*

FOR THE FIRST EIGHT days of Noah's life, his grandfather,
my father-in-law, refused to hold him. He never explained
why, but we knew. We had decided not to celebrate our son's birth
with a brit milah or bris: the ritual circumcision of a newborn boy.
Circumcision is a (or even *the*) fundamental Jewish ritual, spelled
out clearly in Genesis 17:10–14: every male must be circumcised
at eight days old as a sign of the covenant between him and God.
Cut off the foreskin, says God, or cut yourself off from the Jewish
people. In our case, one Jewish person in particular.

The modern American Jewish celebration of this ancient rite
of passage goes something like this: at a small daytime gathering,
an honored person holds the baby, an official (a rabbi or the mohel—the circumciser) says a prayer, and then the mohel slices off
the foreskin of the baby's penis with a quick flick of a knife, a few
prayers, and possibly some antibiotic ointment. The child wails,
the tension breaks, and the guests move on to the brunch buffet.

In one of our first decisions as new parents, my husband and
I declined to throw a party to celebrate our child's ritual mutilation. Does "ritual mutilation" sound extreme? Well, whatever you
think of circumcision, it is mutilation, physically speaking, and it is
ritual mutilation, sociologically speaking—"a means of permanent

differentiation," according to Arnold van Gennep's ethnographic classic, *The Rites of Passage*.

> Cutting off the foreskin is exactly equivalent to pulling out a tooth (in Australia, etc.), to cutting off the little finger just above the last joint (in South America), to cutting off the ear lobe or perforating the ear lobe or the septum, or to tattooing, scarifying, or cutting the hair in a particular fashion.[1]

It wasn't difficult to decide not to have this ceremony, but we felt brave making the decision anyway, knowing we were calling upon ourselves the wrath of Adam's father. A self-described "traditional Jew," he did not tolerate well family members' disobedience, religious or otherwise. He belonged to an Orthodox synagogue, kept a kosher home, and was a stickler for the rules. Almost everyone in his orbit catered to him, worked around him, deceived him, or some combination thereof. Adam and I were more in his orbit than anyone but my mother-in-law: we lived two miles down the road on the family farm, and he stopped by or called half a dozen times a day.

We had predicted that he would be furious when we omitted the ritual that welcomed our child into the Jewish community. We certainly didn't expect that he would not touch his newborn grandson for eight days. Not that Noah noticed. But we did. I should still resent my father-in-law for his stony-faced rejection. Instead, I felt, along with incredulity, an odd kind of pity for him. For his self-defeating attempts to control his grown children's lives. And for being so attached to his rules and his need for control that he sacrificed the pleasure of holding his grandson in his arms.

When he relented after eight days, we guessed that his rabbi had intervened. I could imagine the man shaking his head at a bullheaded congregant who was choosing Mosaic law over love; I could imagine the rabbi sagely inventing a rule about how long a newborn boy is "untouchable" if the parents stray. But it could be that my father-in-law just couldn't stand it anymore. At that point we probably should have refused to hand the child over for an implicit blessing by the very man who had spurned him. Instead, we put the baby in his arms. The world isn't filled with people who are strictly conflict seekers or conflict avoiders. And it's not filled with people acting consistently according to principle or not. It's filled with people deciding how much they can take at any particular moment. We were exhausted from a troubling first week, and we thought we'd made our point.

What point was that exactly? We thought that by not having a ceremonial circumcision we were standing up—in the face of strong parental pressure—against a barbaric and primitive ritual. We thought that by declining the traditional party, by not intoning, in Hebrew, "Blessed are you, Lord our God, king of the universe, who has sanctified us with his commandments and commanded us to enter [Noah] into the Covenant of Abraham our father," we were separating ourselves from our community just as Genesis had warned.

And yet. We *did* have Noah circumcised, in the hospital, the day after he was born. In doing so, we flubbed the "eighth day" timing but otherwise fulfilled our obligations as Jewish parents. The bris—the covenant—has nothing to do with a party or prayers. We still gave our son a "'sign of union' with a particular deity and a mark of membership in a single community of the faithful." We still gave in to the demands of a religion we didn't believe in.

> The mutilated individual is removed from the common mass of humanity by a rite of separation (this is the idea behind cutting, piercing, etc.) which automatically incorporates him into a defined group; since the operation leaves ineradicable traces, the incorporation is permanent.[2]

It's quite possible that my father-in-law finally held his grandson because his rabbi told him not to worry: since the child had been cut, he needn't be cut off.

## THE PAUSE

MY FATHER-IN-LAW ADORED HIS grandchild and behaved from then on as if everything were fine. So we behaved, more or less, as if everything were fine. I'm a get-along kind of girl, which was obviously the reason we got along. My compliance applied to religion, too, and lasted throughout the period when our children were young. On holidays, we polished all three to a high shine and arrived at my in-laws' house with our arms full of round challahs for Rosh Hashanah or flourless desserts for Passover—bringing food in lieu of religious feeling. We never joined a synagogue, and we never attended services, even on High Holidays, when many unobservant Jews flock to the pews. But we hid the fact that we were working when we "should" have been praying, and we told our children not to mention their Yom Kippur playdates when Grandpa inquired about their day.

For years we used the classic avoidance techniques of nonbelievers in religious families. You don't tell your Muslim parents that you drink beer sometimes, and they know enough not to ask. You let your Catholic grandmother assume that you're going to Mass at the college chapel. You eat beef, except when you're with your Hindu relatives. It's a nondisclosure pact, a delicate truce based on avoiding the truth. My father-in-law perhaps imagined that we were headstrong, habitually antagonistic smart alecks who deep down felt a connection to Judaism that would prevail when we matured. But we knew ourselves to be atheists with a growing distaste for the rituals associated with religion who were keeping the peace (more or less) by playing the part when we had to. While these two notions appeared to coexist on parallel tracks, they were in fact bound to collide at another rite of passage: the bar mitzvah.

## THREE OPTIONS

AT THE AGE OF thirteen, Jewish children officially become children (*b'nai*) of the commandment (*mitzvah*) and adults in their community. As Noah steadily approached this magic number, the question arose: Would he have a bar mitzvah ceremony when he came of age?

Even people who knew us well thought that he might. We had, after all, appeared to participate in Jewish life. And although Noah himself was not a believer, he was emphatically a belonger. When Grandpa suggested Noah take Hebrew lessons at their house with a kindly Jewish educator, Noah said, "Sure," and even wore a yarmulke. He knew how to play his part. When aunts and uncles and family friends asked about his upcoming bar mitzvah, he played along.

But what were we actually going to do?

A rite of passage is a culturally or religiously prescribed observance of a change in your life or your status—a bar mitzvah when you become a Jewish adult, a confirmation when you officially join the church, a wedding when you become a husband or wife. But it's also a moment when you publicly declare your relationship to your community. Do you marry in the church or at city hall? Do you baptize your child? Do you rent a tux and go to prom or spend your evening getting stoned and watching *Life of Brian*?

Do you belong? Affirm or deny.

Let's say you are expected to participate in a rite of passage that you don't totally endorse. You have three options.

**Option 1: Participate outwardly but not inwardly.** That is how I treated my own bat mitzvah ceremony. I performed my part, and I enjoyed performing it, but internally I rejected the religious significance of the rite. In this behavior, apparently, I was being very . . . Scandinavian. Although the Scandinavian countries are the most secular societies in the world, most of their citizens, according to sociologist Phil Zuckerman, still get married in church, baptize their children, and get confirmed—all without believing. Zuckerman reports in *Society without God* that he asked one mother what she says to her children when they ask about God. She replied, "I tell them that's bull."[3] But she still had them baptized. He describes a typical Danish wedding in which

> the bride and groom are united under the auspices of a pastor, within the hallowed walls of an old church, amidst invocations of God and Jesus. And yet even some minimal investigating will reveal that hardly anyone believes in a literal God or that Jesus is up in heaven blessing their union—not the bride, not the groom, not the majority of those in attendance, and maybe not even the pastor herself.[4]

Fifty-one percent of Norwegians say they do not believe in God, and another 20 percent say they're not sure,[5] but more than half of all Norwegians[6] are officially confirmed in the church at age fifteen. This rite of passage was a legal and religious requirement between 1736 and 1912—you had to do it to be considered an adult. It's still a big day in a Norwegian adolescence, complete with traditional garb, feasting, and presents. Since 1951, though, Norwegians have had a choice: the traditional religious confirmation, the *kristelig konfirmasjon*, or a *humanistisk konfirmasjon*, for which they complete an ethics course on human rights and critical thinking. You might assume that in a majority nonbelieving nation, a humanist confirmation that celebrates adolescents having "reflected on [their] own opinions and values" would be the preferred option. But in fact the majority of families with fifteen-year-olds choose the ceremony in which a pastor says things (in Norwegian) such as, "Eternal God, heavenly Father, we . . . pray that you show the paths to faith to our confirmation candidates, so that they daily might turn to you, and throughout their lives thus learn to know your son Jesus Christ."[7] Given that younger generations tend more toward nonbelief than the parents who answered the surveys and who organize the ceremonies, this means that a lot of young people are kneeling in pretty *kirker* looking like faithful young Lutherans, while in their heads they are saying (if my Norwegian is correct) *bla bla bla*.

That's essentially what I did at Temple Beth El at age thirteen, intoning, "Blessed is the Eternal One, Giver of the Torah," along with dozens of other prayers addressed to a god that I definitely did not believe was listening. One of my favorite prayers to chant was "*Gadlu l'Adonai iti, un'rom'mah sh'mo yachdav*," which happens to mean, "Declare with me the greatness of God and let us exalt God's name together." Not only was I saying aloud things I didn't believe in, but I was also urging an entire congregation to join me—although many of them probably felt the same. In fact, Zuckerman likens Scandinavian attitudes toward their Lutheran rites of passage to those of many American Jews, for whom the bris, the bar mitzvah, and the wedding under a huppah are primarily about cultural belonging and only secondarily about belief. He imagines a synagogue scene in which "hardly anyone in attendance—including the Jewish teenager and his parents, and probably even the rabbi—sincerely believes in the literal content of what is being said, recited, and sung."[8]

We can interview modern Scandinavians and Reform Jews to confirm our suspicion that what one believes and how one behaves in ritual occasions are two very separate things. But what should we think about the beliefs of people we can't survey? Van Gennep's *The Rites of Passage* details dozens (and lists hundreds) of rituals from around the world, but he does not describe what's going on in the heads of the people who were performing those rites. Perhaps the girl in a traditional Palestinian marriage rite who "approaches her future husband's house carrying a jar full of water on her head, and he makes the jar fall at the moment when the girl straddles the threshold"[9] takes it all very seriously and feels the emotional significance of the "separation from the old environment and incorporation into the new one by a sort of baptism." Or perhaps she's annoyed at having to go along with the charade and makes sure the jar of water isn't quite as full— or as cold—as it could be. Second-century philosopher Sextus Empiricus, debating the existence of the gods, pointed out that merely honoring them in practice did not mean honoring them in belief. He gives the example of the Skeptic, who "performs everything that conduces to their worship and veneration, while at the same time he is by no means hasty in the matter of philosophic inquiry concerning them."[10]

The notion that belief might diverge from behavior appears across cultures and eras. In *Anna Karenina*, Levin, an agnostic, must confess and receive the sacrament in order to get married.

> During the service he would sometimes listen to the prayers, trying to see in them a meaning which would not clash with his opinions, or, finding that he could not understand and had to disapprove of them, he would try not to listen but to occupy his mind with observation of what was going on or with recollections which passed with extraordinary clearness through his brain as he stood idly in the church.[11]

Levin "felt awkward and ashamed at doing something incomprehensible and therefore—as an inner voice told him—necessarily false and wrong." But then when it's all over "he felt as pleased as a dog that was being taught to jump through a hoop, and which, having accomplished what was demanded of it, barks and wags its tail and jumps for joy."[12]

Jumping through that hoop is what philosopher Kwame Anthony Appiah calls "orthopraxy"—or correct behavior. He explains that it's "a matter not of *believing* right," which we know as orthodoxy (correct belief), "but of *acting* right."[13] Acting right is Option 1.

**Option 2: Participate, but with caveats.** We were determined to put our own stamp on our wedding, which was the first rite of passage I truly felt I controlled. We wrote our own vows. We rewrote the traditional Seven Blessings, leaving God out entirely. We dispensed with the tradition of the bride circling the groom seven times and made one up in which our guests passed our wedding rings from hand to hand and finally to us. But we kept the rings. We kept the huppah (the wedding canopy, which was quilted by my big sister and signed by the guests) and the ketubah (the marriage contract) and the rabbi. We kept the stomping of the glass at the end of the ceremony. And thus we kept the celebratory "Mazel Tov!" and the applause that it releases, like so much carbon dioxide chasing a popped cork.

It was, that is, still a recognizably Jewish wedding. Looking back now, it's clear to me that whatever dissenting statements we thought we were making were subsumed in the overarching *assent* of it all.

I recently attended a bar mitzvah service in which the celebrant said, "God's existence doesn't matter to me," and that "He/She/It may exist or may not." He explained that he did not read the Torah as fact or truth but as allegory. The rabbi subsequently praised the child's integrity and ability to stay true to his beliefs (against the rabbi's own attempts to get him to soften his language). And the boy did—refreshingly, even courageously. But he *also* expressed literally the opposite: "May I be a witness to the living God and to God's goodness and to the tradition that lives within me," he said (in English). "In the Torah I have read the word of God. With God's help may I go on to fulfill it in my life."

Even if he'd somehow managed not to praise God explicitly, though, he would have been implicitly signing on, simply by publicly accepting the role of "son of the commandment." So great is the power of traditional ritual that *any* participation implies assent. I was tempted to add another option—*participate, but subvert*—but I realized, no, you just *think* you're subverting. Your bar mitzvah speech can dissect the cruel tyranny of the Old Testament God (I've heard several that do), but, as long as you're participating, you're still assenting. Your graduation mortar board can say "F--- You," but if you're walking across that stage, you're still assenting.

I'm not saying that assent is necessarily a bad thing. Protests from within the structure that religions (or cultures) have decreed push against conformity; they attempt to communicate truth in a way that mere orthopraxy does not. In fact, if you are conflicted or ambivalent, they may be the most honest option, in which you are saying both *yes* and *no*—and you genuinely mean both. *I practice but I don't believe. I value part of this but not all.*

But if you choose Option 2, try to be honest with yourself. I wasn't, as a bride. I didn't admit to myself until later that merely participating in a traditional rite reinforces the rite itself and therefore the culture or religion that prescribes it. Even cockeyed participation endorses the expectation that *this is what one does.* As I wrote in *A Walk Down the Aisle*, "Unfortunately for someone who wants to marry untraditionally, altering the traditional wedding ceremony is itself a hallowed wedding tradition."[14]

**Option 3: Just say no.** The nuclear option. Courting family crisis. Risking schism. Carrying the logic of nonbelief to its behavioral conclusion. Ending the cycle.

In *Society without God*, Zuckerman describes meeting Konrad, a rare Swede who declined a confirmation ceremony, which, like the Norwegian one, is highly popular and ingrained in the culture, even though Swedes are even less likely to believe in God. Most of the Scandinavians we meet in Zuckerman's book choose to celebrate religious rites "not in a state of mere indifference to the supernatural beliefs that underlie them but even while in direct disagreement with them."[15] But Konrad is different, part of a minority who "couldn't reconcile their lack of faith with overt religious involvement."[16] He believed getting confirmed would be hypocritical. As he tells Zuckerman,

In my class in school there was only me and the class punk rocker who didn't get confirmed. I thought, well I don't believe in that, so why should I? Not many of the other kids believed in it either, but they were promised gifts and stuff from their parents if they did. So they only did it because of the gifts. And I thought: that's stupid. I don't believe in that—anything in that—so why should I?[17]

I don't know what that kid's parents thought or whether his friends teased him or how much money Swedes give children upon the occasion of their confirmation. I haven't seen the expensive and ornate traditional garb my Norwegian friend's grandparents gave her in anticipation of the big day, which, she tells me, ensured her own appearance in church. I do know that it's unusual at that age—at any age—to take your own principles seriously enough to say no.

When I was thirteen, as directed by my parents, I picked Option 1: orthopraxy. I acted the model bat mitzvah, an earnest and eager participant in the celebration of my entry into Jewish adulthood. When I was twenty-seven, a thoughtful young bride, my groom and I picked Option 2: alteration. We kept the structure of the Jewish wedding intact and just filled it with our own words. When I was thirty, feeling braver as the defender of my newborn child, I and my husband inadvertently picked Option 2 again: we had our child circumcised, as Judaism required, but in a new and improved setting.

When I was forty-three, my son gave me one last shot at Option 3.

## THE BAR MITZVAH

DESPITE MY MISGIVINGS, I was honestly willing to let Noah decide, in the face of his potential rite of passage, whether he wanted to accept, alter, or decline it. The place of the bar mitzvah in pop culture is legendary: if Noah became a sitcom writer or a standup comedian, he'd have an extra store of material to enrich such American rite-of-passage tropes as Spring Break, Prom, and the Driver's License Test. I had enjoyed my performance as a bat mitzvah, and I was glad I'd done it. If he truly wanted to have that experience, too, could I refuse? Even if he just wanted to be like his cousins? Even if he just wanted the cash?

So I asked him in private if he really wanted to have a bar mitzvah ceremony. He said, "I guess so." I pressed—but why? He replied, "Because I'm Jewish." Which is doubtless the unspoken impetus behind all kinds of rituals, but it hardly indicated sincere desire. It meant he was doing it because he thought he was supposed to, and that wasn't enough for me. Not anymore. So at some point that year, losing sleep and failing to get my husband to lose an equal amount of sleep, I had the brilliant idea of putting the problem back on Noah.

I told him that even though his dad and I didn't believe in any of this stuff, and even though having a bar mitzvah would be a lot of work, we would consider doing it. But first I needed him to write a paragraph explaining why he wanted to.

Just a paragraph. To see if he was serious. To understand his thinking. To show him I would expect effort from him, that *his* desire would be animating this adventure, not mine. I knew how easy it was for him to bare-minimum his good grades or pull a shiny piano recital out of a shabby practice hat. If I put a bar mitzvah in motion, he would go along with it, and he would expend the least amount of intellectual and emotional effort necessary to reap the promised reward. It was an approach to life I respected in theory but couldn't truly endorse. So I decided if there were to be a bar mitzvah, he would have to be the one to put it in motion. If he wanted to choose Option 1 or 2, I would let him, but he would have to make some effort to opt in.

Noah never did opt in. In fact, after a spate of bar mitzvah parties—he was young for his grade, so his few Jewish friends went first, as did his older cousins—he seemed to lose interest, leaving the whole question behind him as he ran happily into his first season on the cross-country team. "I guess so" became "I guess not." His thirteenth birthday passed. My father-in-law made no comment. I had, I thought, miraculously sidestepped a rite of passage without ever explicitly saying no to it.

One evening in November, a month after he turned thirteen, I took Noah up to his grandparents' house for another of those sporadic Hebrew lessons with a private teacher. In my head, bringing Noah for these lessons was a sort of peace offering. We didn't go to synagogue—or let our kids go with their grandfather when he asked—and our children didn't go to religious school. And now our son had turned thirteen without a corresponding Jewish ceremony. I had won without even having to fight. So I could graciously accept some free foreign language instruction. A bit of Hebrew couldn't hurt his brain. Well-educated people should be familiar with the Old Testament. And an hour of tutoring every once in a while didn't seem like too much to ask if it would make an old man happy. This was my reasoning in the face of my husband's *this-can't-end-well* head shaking.

Adam was right. When I went to pick up Noah, my father-in-law informed me that they had chosen his Torah portion and set a date. "He's not having a bar mitzvah," I said, incredulous. "Yes, I am," said Noah. My brain froze. "We'll talk about this at home," said my face. But it didn't take even that three-minute drive to squeeze out of Noah his reasoning. "I thought you weren't interested in a bar mitzvah! Why would you have one?" He said, "It would make Grandpa happy."

He meant it. Noah was sweet at his core, and, despite the lawyering, almost always did what he was asked. He was also attached to his grandpa. Did he really want to have a bar mitzvah ceremony? Did he want to study Torah? Did he believe that God was anything other than a character? Did he intend to participate in a Jewish community? No, no, no, and no. But he wasn't ready to aim those nos at Grandpa, risking disappointment, disapproval, and possibly disfavor.

Noah was then thirteen, but he was still my baby, still under my protection and control. Becoming bar mitzvah means (or once meant) assuming the legal responsibilities of adulthood, both religious (countable as a member of a prayer group) and legal (eligible to buy property, liable for his crimes). But *until* that point, he's still a child. That's why the traditional prayer of the bar mitzvah's father is the very heartwarming "Blessed be He who has released me from being punishable for this boy."[18] Before he is bar mitzvah, he is still our responsibility.

I asked Noah if he wanted me to tell Grandpa that there would be no bar mitzvah. He said yes, but only if I promised not to say the decision was coming from him. I promised: I would be the punishable one, not he.

### CHOOSING OPTION 3

*YOU DON'T HAVE TO explain.* That's what I kept reminding myself after I resolved to tell my father-in-law that his grandson would not be celebrating a bar mitzvah.

*Just say it's not going to happen. Don't say anything else.*

He knew well enough that we were not religious—that's why he had been bringing Noah up to his house to meet with a Hebrew tutor. And that's why he didn't even speak to his son or me (a.k.a. Noah's parents) before deciding that Noah was going to be bar mitzvah. You don't sneak around someone you think agrees with you.

So my no would be a blow, but not a shock. And trying to soften that blow—with explanations, justifications, apologies—might simply confuse the matter. I had to be clear. He had been relying on my get-along personality for more than two decades by then. Clearly, he'd assumed that if he just took charge and planned a bar mitzvah for his grandson, we'd go along with it. I had *taught* him to assume that. To be sure, in order to preserve my self-respect, I had redirected Passover seders to focus on civil rights; I'd made God gender neutral (or worse) in English when even I could read Hebrew well enough to know he was male; I'd gotten married in a renovated dairy barn instead of a synagogue. But these nos, I now realized, had been whispers, prevarications, maybes, even implicit yeses. Even no to the ceremonial bris thirteen years before had been, fundamentally, a yes—yes to circumcision, yes to forgiveness for his religiously motivated bad behavior, and yes to peace above principle.

Now, for my son, but really for me, I had to say no.

It fell to me and not to my husband because (1) I had gotten us into this pickle by taking Noah for Hebrew lessons and engaging in other acts of appeasement, and (2) I thought I could reduce the chance of total catastrophe, be that a massive fight or eviction from our house on the family farm that Adam ran. His father owned the property and, when he felt his authority was being challenged, relished threatening us with eviction as a movie strongman relishes flashing a gun. But he'd never threatened *me* before, only Adam.

Of course, the reason he had never threatened me personally might have been that I had never directly opposed him. So I was nervous. And oddly, although he usually stopped by several times a day, it was a week after he announced that our son was having a bar mitzvah before I saw him again. He came into the kitchen without knocking, as usual, and, as usual, asked about our chickens' current egg production. I answered. And then I said, with the counter between us and with my heart pounding, "It's fine for Noah to be learning some Hebrew, but he is not going to have a bar mitzvah."

His eyes narrowed. "What's going on here?"

All my careful reasoning swirled through my careful head. All the things I could say. *At best, it would be meaningless for Noah to celebrate a bar mitzvah; at worst, it would be dishonest. Noah can bond with his grandpa in other ways. He can always become bar mitzvah as a grown-up if he so chooses. Furthermore, according to Jewish rules, he already is "bar mitzvah" (son of the commandment)—just turning thirteen does that. No party required.*

Not to mention the most fundamental reason of all: reason.

*I'm not letting my son stand up in a synagogue to praise an imaginary being and officially undertake to uphold the laws of a people who worship Him—even though he doesn't believe in the being or subscribe to the laws.*

There are 613 Jewish commandments, and none of them says that my son had to celebrate a bar mitzvah. But my refusing this rite of passage on my son's behalf would nevertheless break plenty of them, from "To know there is a God" (number one) to "To learn Torah and teach it to your sons" (number 22) to "Honor" (number 584) and "Fear" (number 585) your father and mother and "Not to be a rebellious son" (number 586, granting some gender leeway). Obviously, I did not subscribe to these laws any more than I did to number 598: "Wipe out the descendants of Amalek."[19] And yet, I somehow still felt guilty for breaking them. In the face of my father-in-law's disapproval, I wanted to explain, excuse, and exonerate myself. I was that uncomfortable being in the wrong, even if "the wrong" I was in was actually right.

I remember jogging with my father once in Spain and feeling terribly unnerved not (or not only) because the street cops carried submachine guns, but because the old ladies hissed at the sight of my bare legs in running shorts. I was twelve years old. I knew there was nothing *actually* wrong with baring my legs, but I still hated that anyone might think I was in the wrong. Later, visiting my Italian relatives, I was deeply embarrassed when my cousin, an observant Jew, found me writing a letter on a Saturday; writing is working, and I wasn't supposed to be working on the sabbath. I never ordered pork when out to dinner with my father-in-law, even though it wasn't I who kept kosher, and I would blush and yammer if he dropped by during the week of Passover while I was making the kids a not-matzoh (and therefore not permissible) sandwich.

It was crazy to feel guilt, shame, or even discomfort when I broke the rules of religions to which I did not subscribe. There is no moral basis for these rules, and, since there is no God-who-disapproves-of-bare-legs-or-leavened-bread outside our collective imagination, there is no basis for them at all. None.

It was likewise crazy that—absent belief, absent observance, absent participation in Jewish life, absent parental input—Noah's bar mitzvah was the expected thing and that *not* doing it required an explanation.

It was backward. But we live in a backward world, where there's a special name for people who do not grant the existence of a creature that no one can see or hear or prove exists. We atheists—the ones who have not signed on to a completely speculative story about the way the world works—are the ones who are strange and suspect. And we get used to pretending we do (or might) believe, and we get used to soft-pedaling our disbelief or apologizing for it. We get used to going along with it to get along with everyone.

A backward world.

Standing in my kitchen, I made the tiniest effort to set it right.

"What's going on here?" he asked again.

"Noah is not going to bar mitzvah," I said. It was that simple.


## CROSSING A THRESHOLD

FOR ABOUT A YEAR after I said no to Noah's bar mitzvah, I tried to think of a way to give him a religion-free adolescent rite of passage. I wanted to celebrate the transition away from the self-centeredness of childhood to the social awareness of adulthood. At least that's how I saw the difference, while my children still routinely forgot they weren't alone in public places. "Other human beings!" was my recurring reminder at the grocery store whenever their voices and bodies spilled past polite boundaries. When would they start to understand themselves as part of a society? When would they start to accept responsibility for their behavior and its effect on others? *That* would be a change worth celebrating.

A rite of passage not only celebrates this transition but also helps create it. After all, the bar mitzvah happens whether or not a child is physically, emotionally, or intellectually ready for the responsibilities of adulthood. That's why it's played for laughs in the movies and on television: a set of orthodontia in an ill-fitting suit squeakily declaring (in the common formulation), "Today I am a man." Obviously, the boy is not, but just maybe the bar mitzvah nudges him in that direction. Forsaking fun for extra studying, interacting with teachers one-on-one, greeting guests, making your cousins feel included in your friend group, thanking gift givers—the whole bar mitzvah apparatus in some ways *makes* rather than marks the change in perspective from child to adult.

The trick would be to find a rite that was more honest than a bar mitzvah, more unusual than a piano recital, and more communal than reading a list of classic novels. I've got it, I thought: he should host a dinner party! Dinner parties were a fixture of my kids' childhood; they were how Adam and I got through long evenings with young kids. Cooking nice meals for a tableful of guests was more hectic but far more entertaining than just slogging it out on the floor with a train set until—thank God—bath time. The kids were pretty good at their kid-sized tasks, such as putting out the appetizers before the guests arrived and not eating the appetizers before the guests arrived. But wouldn't it be a worthy rite of passage if Noah had to plan, make, serve, and clean up after dinner, too? We could call him a *bar mitbach*, son of the kitchen. The child would learn skills, feel accomplished, and be the center of attention. His guests would confer upon him their compliments and blessings and bring him presents or charitable donations instead of the usual bottle of wine. He could make a bar mitbach toast instead of a bar mitzvah speech, and his parents could toast, too, tears welling up as we spoke with pride about our beautiful boy and his mastery of the basic vinaigrette, about how, of course—you know Noah (we'd roll our fond eyes)—he had to put his own spin on creamed spinach.

That's how I daydreamed it, anyway. It never came to pass. Noah wasn't interested, and I didn't have the energy and the conviction to make him do it. Looking back, I wish I had. It's true that giving dinner parties was an essential part of what *I* thought a grown-up should be. If I'd made him do it, he might well have just gone through the motions while the running commentary in his head said *blah blah blah*. The whole experience might not have sunk in at all. He might have made a fine dinner, impressed his guests, and then returned immediately to his adolescent stance of doing-exactly-what's-asked-of-him-and-no-more just as a bar mitzvah boy might stop going to synagogue, forget his Hebrew letters, and abandon his service project the moment he was free. He might have merely catered to my value system, trapped as he was in my care.

I worried that making him do anything was too much like having him bar mitzvah against his beliefs, but I think I was wrong. It's different. I said no to a bar mitzvah not because I didn't want to impose *my* beliefs on my children, but because I didn't want to impose *someone else's*.

Of course, my beliefs didn't spring fully formed from inside my head. They are influenced by my upbringing and my culture in ways I probably don't fully understand. But by age forty-three, I felt I had thought about them enough to decide which ones I was willing to stand by and act on. One of those was the right to choose some and reject others, no matter how many generations before me had accepted them. *That* was the belief I most wanted to pass on. If Noah had been bar mitbach, he might or might not have fully digested my dinner-party values, but he would have internalized the value of raising children the way you think is right, not the way other people do. Not the way your parents or their parents or your neighbors do. He would have fully appreciated the truth and beauty of Option 3 and would have been prepared, when his time came, to make his kids not give a dinner party, maybe, but organize a camping trip or a film festival. And he would know how to make a vinaigrette.

As it is, with no public rite of passage, Noah did the work of becoming a grown-up on his own, as many people do. He crossed not one public ceremonial threshold from one life stage to another but a hundred private ones. Not by external rites, but by internal shifts of experience and understanding, some universal and some individual, and most of which he wouldn't recognize for years to come. When he first drove a car by himself. When he first fell in love. When he first navigated a train station or an airport alone. When he first stepped in to help a parent who was sick. When he first had sex. When he first learned a family secret. When he first saw himself from the perspective of someone he'd mistreated.

"First" is key here, a universal distinction. Van Gennep describes the differences in the rites for a first child as opposed to subsequent children, a first marriage as opposed to a second, "the first haircut, the first tooth, the first solid food, the first step, the first menses."[20] You can cross each threshold only once. So it was, too, that I had to say no only for Noah. No one suggested that our second son or our daughter become b'nai mitzvah. "The magic circle is broken for the first time," says van Gennep, "and, for that individual, it can never again be completely closed."[21]

After all the dread and the internal debate and the below-surface drama, it was indeed as simple as saying no. We were not thrown out of the house. Noah was not ejected from his grandpa's favor. The relationship was strained for a while, and then it wasn't. But something had shifted, in me at least. At age forty-three, I had crossed a threshold: I had finally made my behavior match my beliefs.

# UNPLUGGING FROM
# THE HIGHER POWER

*For mortal to aid mortal—this is god.*
PLINY THE ELDER, *Natural History*

W E PARKED IN THE lot next to a lone car and, once inside, wound our way through the seemingly empty church in search of the basement door. I hung close to my friend, my guide to the world of Alcoholics Anonymous. I wanted to know what AA was like, and what his new life was like, so when he was headed to a meeting during a weekend visit to our house, I asked to go with him.

I regretted the outing as soon as we found the room. I had seen enough "meeting" scenes in movies to picture rows of folding chairs half filled with reluctant people clutching coffee cups and coats. I imagined a lectern up front and myself in the back row at a friendly, supportive remove. Instead, we were the fourth and fifth people to arrive, and we draped our coats around chairs set in an intimate circle. I smiled nervously at the three other people, wondering what I would say when it was my time to address them. I had seen that in the movies, too. "Hi, I'm Kate, and I'm _____"? Oh, good: two more arrived; now we were seven. Nine. Ten. At the last minute, the circle filled, and we were twelve.

The AA recovery program is structured as a series of twelve steps. The first thing we did, after the opening welcome, was read the steps out loud, one by one, from a photocopied sheet in a plastic sleeve, passing them from person to person. When my friend handed them to me, I handed them right along to the fellow on my right. As a visitor, I didn't feel like it was my place to say them. As an atheist, I didn't think I could.

I had known before I came that AA traditionally asks its members to cede control of their lives to a Higher Power, so I figured there would be a God-related step or two. But it's much more than that. This is not an "I accept these terms and conditions" check-the-box situation. This is not bowing your head respectfully while someone else says grace. Six of the twelve steps of the program involve God, from "Came to believe that a power greater than ourselves could restore us to sanity" (Step 2) to "Humbly asked him to remove our shortcomings" (Step 7) to "Sought through prayer and meditation to improve our conscious contact with God, as we understood Him, praying only for knowledge of His will for us and the power to carry that out" (Step 11). Even the God who peacocked through four of the Ten Commandments would be impressed.

After we read the steps, the meeting became less about God and more like church. We passed out copies of the Big Book (*Alcoholics Anonymous*, the AA "bible")—fat black hardbacks fetched from a cabinet under the coffee maker. There was some discussion about where the group had left off, and then we settled in to read "Stars Don't Fall," a testimonial by Felicia G., who drank her way through the 1940s before eventually grasping sobriety.

As we read her story aloud, turn by turn, paragraph by paragraph, we were implicitly tasked with finding commonality between her story and ours. It wasn't easy. Felicia wasn't just from a different era, in which one went to "gin mills" to get "tight," she was from a different life entirely. She was born in a castle, had a chalet in Switzerland, and kept a house in Virginia during fox-hunting season.

But when she describes her preoccupation with drink, even I, a "normal," possessed of what AA refers to as the "power of choice in drink," could relate:

Other girls whom I had known all my life asked for one weak scotch after dinner. Sometimes they'd put it on the mantel, and forget it. My eye would be glued to that glass. How could anybody *forget* a drink?

That's a feeling I knew, more or less, from craving food: I had watched in wonder as waiters cleared plates that still had French fries on them. It wasn't the same, but all the same, I recognized it, and I began to see Felicia and feel her struggles.

First she tries to stop drinking on her own—"I must use self-will, self-control. I must go on the wagon for a while"—but she fails. She cannot do it alone. Eventually her analyst sends her to Bill (AA's founder), who sends her to Marty, who takes her to a meeting, and soon she meets Priscilla, who asks her to help Anne, who is in real trouble. One night, when Anne desperately needs help, Felicia calls the AA central office, which dispatches John and Bud to meet them. "They did not seem ashamed to be with us, these strangers. They were taking the trouble to try and help. Why? I was astonished and deeply moved."

"I think now," writes Felicia, "that a God, in whom I did not believe, was looking after me."

At this point, I wanted to raise my hand, as if I were in class rather than in church. God? Really? As far as I could tell, Felicia had just movingly described who was actually looking after her: Bill and Marty and Priscilla and John and Bud and so on. Looking around the room at these people patiently listening to one another, serving each other coffee and cookies, passing information from hand to hand, and ultimately—in the few minutes left after the reading was over—sharing their stories with the group, I could see clearly what the real "Higher Power" was: human power in disguise. Not that these people didn't believe in God, in one way or another. Even my friend, an atheist like me, was trying to figure out whether he could at least make the switch to agnostic. And yet the source of their salvation was clearly *them*, not Him. "I, alone and unaided, could not stop" drinking, writes Felicia. So she gets help from other human beings—and gives God the credit.

I can understand the appeal of consigning your rescue to something larger than yourself. If you'd reached a point where your life was out of control, you might well despair at the notion that you are responsible for taking control of it again. And you might not be able or willing to ask others for help: you might not trust them or you might not think you deserve their kindness and generosity. AA's focus on the Higher Power is, perhaps unintentionally, a brilliant feat of misdirection: *Look—up there—that will save you, that will hold you up—and, whoops, steady there, here, take my hand . . .*

"Things get a little better when we ask for help," writes Anne Lamott in her book about prayer. Then she adds—and, I think, clarifies: "People help us."[1]


## "GOD LOVES CLEVELAND"

GOD GETS CREDIT FOR all sorts of things people do in America, even things you wouldn't think he'd have much interest in. When the Cavaliers beat the Golden State Warriors in the 2016 NBA final, coming back from a 3-to-1 deficit and ending a three-sport citywide championship drought that had lasted fifty-two years, Dan Gilbert, owner of the Cavs, told a reporter, "God loves Cleveland, Ohio."[2]

Giving God credit for athletic success is the absurd end of the Higher Power spectrum. The idea that God has an interest in one's personal life—let alone one's personal *entertainment*—seems like the height of self-absorption and even callousness. Let's say we were believers and thought God was on our side. Why would we *want* a Supreme Being who spends time deciding the NBA final when at any moment somewhere in the world a mother is digging desperately through rubble for her child?

While God often gets credit for a win, few blame him (publicly, at least) for a team loss. I would love to see that.

COURTSIDE REPORTER
You were twenty-two points ahead at the end of the half. What
do you think went wrong today?

COACH
I have to say, Bob, we had a really strong pre-game prayer circle, so I kind of thought we'd pull this one out. Truth is, I'm
disappointed in the Big Guy.

I have to admit: Clevelanders were unusual in that they actually
*did* blame God for decades of failure; "GodHatesCleveland" is a
popular Cleveland Browns fan blog. And after the win, the *Onion*
published an article entitled, "God Clarifies That He Still Hates
Cleveland Fans Despite Cavaliers Championship."

Occasionally, God makes athletes lose not out of spite but for
the athlete's own good. The astonishing gymnast Simone Biles reflected thus on one of her rare failures: "I didn't make the [2011]
National team so I was super upset about that but I knew that it
was God's way of telling me I needed to go home, train harder, so
that next year I could make it happen."[3] Put another way, not making the national team was God's way of telling her she would have
to train harder to make the national team—exactly what a person
might logically conclude from . . . not making the team.

Biles is not the first Olympian to believe that a divinity took an
interest in her athletic feats. The original Olympics, the ancient
Greek athletic games that started in the eighth century BCE, were
featured events at festivals held to honor Zeus. Before the contests
began, each competitor prayed to Zeus and swore by him to follow
the rules. Afterward, there was a procession to the temple, where
the victors, wearing wreaths of sacred plants, made "dedications to
the gods."[4] Did they think the gods could affect the outcome of the
games? Classicist Sarah Murray, writing about religion in Greek
sport, thinks at least some did. She cites the "curse tablets" that show

athletes asking the gods to hobble their opponents. "Bind Eurychian in the unilluminated eternity of oblivion," reads one, "and chill and destroy also the wrestling that he is going to do this coming Friday."[5] And in his odes to the victors of the games, the fifth-century-BCE poet Pindar gave the presiding god as much or more credit than the athlete himself. A victorious boxer may have "done valiantly with his fists" but it's "Father Zeus" who "holdest sway."[6]

Greek religion "was based more on practice than on belief,"[7] says Murray. The practice part—what they said and did—is the only part we know about two-plus millennia later. Regardless of what the Olympians actually believed, they were participating in an explicitly religious rite. When athletes praise God now, though, in the secular context of the Chase Center or Yankee Stadium, they are not doing it because they have to. So why do they?

With athletes, as with anyone who talks about God in public, I see three possible answers.

(1) They sincerely believe that God made them and their talents, and that accepting praise for those talents would be wrong. "We can't take credit for this," Olympic silver medal diver David Boudia told NBC Sports. "To God be the glory."[8] Yankee pitcher Mariano Rivera: "Everything I have and everything I became is because of the strength of the Lord, and through him I have accomplished everything."[9] They have been blessed, and they want to acknowledge that. Or else they see every flawless double back handspring on beam as a kind of hymn of praise. Like the ancient Greeks, they interpret athletic feats to be "suitable gifts for the immortals."[10]

(2) They need to say *something*. The postgame interview is the only thing standing between them and a shower, and rote references to God give them something easy and uncontroversial to say. Something premade they can just pop in the microwave. As in the "Learn Your Clichés" scene in Bull Durham, when veteran Crash teaches rookie Nuke how to do an interview: "Write it down. 'I just wanna give it my best shot and, the good Lord willing, things will work out.'"[11]

So athletes may mean it—they really do think God deserves credit, at least in a larger sense, for their run of three-pointers—or they may just be mouthing comfortable, convenient pieties that no one will question. But there's also a third possibility:

(3) They have strong feelings—such as humility and transcendence—for which they don't have better words. Pointing heavenward, whether physically or rhetorically, deflects praise and attention; it points away from oneself. It's almost the opposite of being so self-absorbed that you think God cares about your ballgame; it's an expression of humility. Maybe some athletes don't want to take credit for being luckier or better than others. Or maybe the moment feels bigger than they are, an event more cosmic than athletic. The big win, the great play, even their own crazy talent, makes them feel small and full of wonder. So they point to God as a way of pointing to that feeling of transcendence.

"What goes into a streak like this?" ESPN reporter Doris Burke asked Kevin Durant in 2014 after yet another NBA game in which he scored more than thirty points. "God," he replied. "That's all I can say. Jesus Christ." Burke paused, laughed lightly, and persisted: "You had nothing to do with it?"

"No. It's all Him."[12]

## ORDINARY MIRACLES

WHATEVER THE MOTIVE—belief, cliché, humility—giving God credit for an NBA championship seems harmless enough. But giving God credit for more serious things can be more of a problem. Take the case of Mott Hall Bridges Academy, a small middle school in a high-poverty Brooklyn neighborhood. Its founder, Nadia Lopez, was principal for ten years, during which time she personally attempted to empower every student in her school. This is what she said about why the school color is purple, the color of royalty:

> I want my scholars to know that even if they live in a housing
> project, they are part of a royal lineage going back to great
> African kings and queens. They belong to a group of individ-
> uals who invented astronomy and math. And they belong to a
> group of individuals who have endured so much history and
> still overcome. When you tell people you're from Brownsville,
> their face cringes up. But there are children here that need to
> know that they are expected to succeed.[13]

I know about Lopez thanks to Vidal Chastanet, one of her students, who was featured in photographer Brandon Stanton's *Humans of New York* series. Stanton asked Vidal who had influenced
him the most in his life, and Vidal answered, "my principal," so
Stanton went in search of her. Thanks to *Humans of New York*,
Lopez's fame spread, not just to me but also to Ellen DeGeneres
and President Obama. And thanks to Lopez's own inspirational
work and the human need to be inspired and, once inspired, to
act, Mott Hall Bridges received almost a million-and-a-half dol-
lars in donations.

For all of this, Lopez gives credit to God.

> I was ready to quit, I was ready to resign, I was done, and my
> mother told me to pray on it . . . I did pray about it Monday,
> and God showed me how much of a significance I was, not
> only to Vidal but to people around the world who could iden-
> tify what it was like to know someone who was their champion
> and pushed them through.[14]

It's not like $1.4 million just showed up on the doorstep. It's not
like people started sending in checks for no evident reason. Cause
and effect are transparently clear in this situation, but still, God
gets credit, if not for the cash itself then for the chain of events that
led people to give. ("You had nothing to do with it?" Doris Burke
might venture to ask.)

The Higher Power can overshadow and even obscure human power. In his podcast "Against the Rules,"[15] author Michael Lewis tells the story of a man named Joe, who fell off a boat off the coast of Southern California in 2014. Joe didn't have a life preserver. He tried to swim to shore but soon realized he was being sucked out to sea. He thought he was going to die. "What he did as he drifted was what people do: he tried to make sense of things," narrates Lewis. Joe, recalling the event, says, "I realized I couldn't do it myself . . . so I called God's name and I started praying to him and he just strengthened me." He had leg cramps, he prepared to "meet his maker," and he started praying harder and harder. And then, eight hours into his ordeal, Joe is rescued by the Coast Guard.

Joe believes this rescue was a miracle. He's grateful to the Coast Guard, but he believes his rescue transpired the way it did "through my Lord Savior Jesus Christ and God." That is the testimony he gave at three churches after he was rescued. And that was the testimony he gave to Lewis. "Whether you believe or not, you guys are talking to a miracle right now."

Lewis doesn't argue the point. "We *are* talking to a miracle," he says to the listener. But, he adds, "Two miracles, actually. The other miracle, the ordinary miracle, is Art Allen."

As the oceanographer of the US Coast Guard Office of Search and Rescue, Arthur A. Allen invented a new method of finding people lost at sea. Early in his career he realized that measuring wind and currents wasn't enough; to pinpoint where the ocean had carried a person, you had to calculate drift. So he developed a tool that did just that: the Search and Rescue Optimal Planning System, or SAROPS. From dropping objects into the Long Island Sound and measuring how they moved, he ultimately produced mathematical equations to describe the probable course and speed of sixty-eight different objects at drift. Then, beginning in 2007, he taught Coast Guard units around the country how to use this software to find people they wouldn't have—or find them faster than they might have. The result, as Allen describes it, is that they are "literally pull-

ing people out of the water that would be dead within hours." SA-
ROPS saves about a thousand lives a year. It saved Joe's. But when
Joe tells the story, who gets the credit? God does.

Joe's interpretation of his rescue, like Lopez's interpretation of
her school's good fortune, is relatively unremarkable in the United
States, where it's normal to give God credit for happy endings. If
Mott Hall Bridges were in Scandinavia, though, its principal would
not be publicly thanking God for answering her prayer and helping
her school. For one thing, Scandinavians generally find God talk
embarrassing: In Denmark, a pastor told sociologist Phil Zuckerman, "you would rather go naked through the city than talk about
God."[16] For another thing, a school in Scandinavia would not be
forced to rely on the largesse of strangers who learn about it on
the internet. It would be well and fully funded by the government.

Those two facts—that Scandinavian society is both secular and
socially secure—are related. The more secular a society, the better
off its citizens, as Zuckerman spells out elsewhere:

> The correlation is clear and strong: the more secular tend to
> fare better than the more religious on a vast host of measures,
> including homicide and violent crime rates, poverty rates, obe-
> sity and diabetes rates, child abuse rates, educational attain-
> ment levels, income levels, unemployment rates, rates of sexu-
> ally transmitted diseases and teen pregnancy, etc.[17]

The correlation between secularity and well-being holds not
only country by country (Sweden versus Pakistan), but also state
by state in the United States (Vermont takes better care of its
people than Mississippi does). But are these facts just accidents of
correlation? Or is the connection causal? Zuckerman argues that
greater societal health causes greater secularity—that when people
are healthier, wealthier, and more secure, they are less dependent
on the consolations of religion and the promise of a better life after death. But he acknowledges that it's possible to argue causality

the other way, to make the case that "a minimal focus on God/the afterlife and a stronger focus on solving problems of daily life in a rational, secular manner have led to positive successful societal outcomes in Scandinavia."[18]

That's why it matters when someone gives God the glory that belongs instead to a dogged Coast Guard oceanographer. Misrepresenting the true mechanisms of human flourishing leaves those mechanisms vulnerable to neglect. Art Allen was able to develop SAROPS only because he had Coast Guard resources and funding. Lewis calls the US government "a petri dish for growing expertise." No private company would fund such painstaking and unprofitable research. Experts employed by the federal government, says Lewis, are "people working on problems the free market would never ever solve on its own." If we don't recognize that, if we don't give government the credit for its role in our lives, then we risk undervaluing and thus underfunding the means of our own rescue.

Likewise, concluding that God helped Lopez's school, directly or indirectly, minimizes not just what Lopez herself did but also what Stanton did and what people moved by his story did. I'm sure no one involved, least of all Lopez herself, felt the need to take credit. I understand the impulse toward humility. But minimizing the human role minimizes human responsibility, and it obscures and undermines the very real human systems and actions that actually produce the miracles that believers attribute to divine action. When we as a culture believe a Higher Power is in charge, do we really use *human power* to its fullest? Do we invest as much as we should in the systems that actually do save people's lives? Do we demand that our government find ways to alleviate the suffering of our neighbors? Well, why would we? If God briefly brought attention and good fortune to Mott Hall Bridges, then it's God who usually lets it languish—or God who leaves the school down the road to languish. Poverty and its relief are His doing, not ours.

## HUMAN POWER

IT'S ONE THING TO wish generally for a Scandinavian-style embrace of societal solutions to life problems. It's another thing to realize, on a personal level, that we are responsible for our own lives. But this is the crux of it all, the one step an atheist has to take, by definition. You can reject the notion that God is real but still use religious frameworks for your life events, use religious holidays to disrupt the humdrum of your days, use religious phrasing for your value system, and even use religious buildings and the religious services they host as a spur to periodic contemplation of your life. I promise you: atheists do all of that. I still do some of it.

Don't get me wrong: I think it's worth reconsidering your holidays and your holy spaces—that's why I dedicated chapters to doing just that. I think your life would be richer if it were filled with scratch-made rituals instead of the pre-fab kind. The fact is, though, you *can* use some of the conveniences of religion without actually believing in God.

But if you do not believe in a Supreme Being, you must give up the notion of God's plan, God's will, God's purpose, God's mysterious ways. God's power. There's no way around it. It can be difficult to accept that our lives are in our hands or in no one's—no ultimate authority to thank, beg, or blame. More than difficult: bewildering, upsetting. But accepting that we are responsible for ourselves and one another is perhaps the atheist's highest calling. It's the way our personal metaphysical beliefs can affect the world.

## THOUGHTS AND PRAYERS

FEW AMERICAN EVENTS ARE as grotesque as the massacre of school children by guns. In these moments—I will not contest it—religion appears to offer consolation. Angel Garza said, of his murdered ten-year-old daughter, "My little love is now flying high with the angels above."[19] Part of me hopes all the parents of children lost to gun violence are believers, that, for the rest of their lives, they live in an alternate reality, imagining—no, knowing—that their children continue to live happily after death, watching out for their siblings.

But I hope the rest of us know that's not true. Or at least that we act as if it isn't. Because I've just thought of something more grotesque than a massacre of school children: the *repeated* massacre of school children. Best case, belief in God gives people solace when something terrible happens; worst case, it allows them to shirk their very real responsibilities to one another while offering "thoughts and prayers."

Most people understand that bad religion—religion that preaches hate and shame—has done terrible things, from slaughtering people who worship other gods to enabling sexual predators to withholding condoms in AIDS-ravaged countries. I just watched a video in which a crowd watched a man whip a woman for removing her hijab in public. Two men actually—the first one got tired. Bad religion is responsible for some of the worst things people do to one another.

But what about good religion? What about religion that clearly means no harm, tries to heal the world (or at least a small corner of it), and even inspires people to give up drinking, to start a school for poor students, to stay afloat until the Coast Guard comes, to make it through another grief-wracked day? Bad religion endorsed slavery and sanctified racism, but didn't good religion fight for abolition and lead the Civil Rights Movement?

Yes. Good religion has sometimes led us forward. But in the long run, it could still be holding us back.

We may not want to think about it or to admit it, but we have the power to save not just Mott Hall Bridges but all the schools that struggle to help kids in impoverished areas. We have the power to end poverty. We can end the epidemic of gun massacres. We have the power to regulate gun ownership, to outlaw the civilian possession of military-style weapons, to buy back AR-15s, to hold gun manufacturers financially and legally liable for the carnage. Australia stopped it, New Zealand stopped it, England stopped it, Norway stopped it. But we can't stop it if we believe that a massacre is simply God calling his angels home, if we believe he has a mysterious plan that involves children hiding among their friends' dead bodies to keep from being shot themselves.

We have to believe that what controls the circumstances of one human's life *is humans*—not just individually, but in the systems that we create together. Talking as if God were in charge encourages us to act as if he is. As if the differential between rich schools and poor schools—as if the next school massacre—were not, ultimately, our responsibility.

But they are. The future of kids like Vidal is not in God's hands; it's in Lopez's. It's in ours. The next school massacre will not happen on God's watch. It will happen on ours.

## ACT LIKE AN ATHEIST

BY THE TIME WE went to that AA meeting, my friend had been sober for about a hundred days. His phone was filled with new numbers: other AA members he called to check up on and those who called to check on him. His calendar was filled, too, with meetings and assignments from his sponsor. AA puts you right to work in the service of others: making the coffee, running the meetings, giving literature to new members. "Do you think that you are one of us?" Bill asks Felicia when they first meet. Saying yes included her instantly in a network of people who help one another.

Felicia was saved, it seemed to me, not just by the people helping her but also by her helping them. Serving others gave her a sense of purpose and worth, not to mention a distraction from self-pity and the desire to drink. "I completely forgot about myself," she writes, "in trying vainly to help Anne, whose misery I understood."

That's it, I thought: that's what is saving my friend. Whatever the AA literature says about having to admit "the possible existence of a Creative Intelligence,"[20] whatever people tell themselves when they're in distress and feel that they have messed everything up in their lives, these people were *acting* as if they were responsible for one another. I don't know what they actually believed—you can't tell from the words people recite. I learned later that nontheistic AA members embrace the latitude of "God as we understood him" (Step 3) to mean any "power greater than ourselves" (Step 2), including one another, as in G.O.D.: Group of Drunks. But even if everyone in that room on that day was picturing an anthropomorphic God, they were acting like atheists in the literal sense of the word—people who are without gods, people whom the gods have left to fend for themselves.

As for Principal Lopez, she may believe that God sent reinforcements, but she didn't wait for a higher power to take action, and she didn't accept the way things were for the kids in Brownsville as the way God intended them to be. She took personal responsibility for improving the lives of the students in her care. Like all believers who do good in the world, she was acting like an atheist, too.

Without gods, we have to depend on human power. We can't shake our heads sadly at a tragedy and murmur "mysterious ways" and do nothing to prevent the next one. We must accept the burdens of humanity.

In asking you to embrace your atheism, I won't tell you to stop going to church or stop bowing your head while someone says grace or stop singing Christmas carols. But I will ask you to remember the human power behind things. If the Coast Guard saves you, find out how. If children die senselessly, find out why—and try to stop it. If you need to forget about yourself, help someone else.

# Epilogue
# COMING OUT WITH THE TRUTH

*Are we like the families in which the adults go through*
*all the motions of believing in Santa Claus for the sake of the kids,*
*and the kids all pretend still to believe in Santa Claus*
*so as not to spoil the adults' fun?*

DANIEL DENNETT, *Breaking the Spell*

RELIGION OFFERS SHORTCUTS TO the fulfillment of many human needs: facing mortality, thinking about morality, expressing gratitude, marking the passage of time, and so on. I hope I have shown that such shortcuts are not the only routes and that, in fact, there are advantages to traveling a different path.

If you don't believe in God, you don't have to go through the motions. You can live a full and fulfilling life without religion. In fact, whether or not you ever succeed in praying to Not You, whether or not you discover the perfect secular combination of home and temple, whether or not you find a religion-free holiday that gives you a transcendent sense of connection, I believe your life can be richer, fuller, and more meaningful just for the attempt.

But couldn't you do all that in the privacy of your own home? Is there any reason you need to tell other people that you don't believe in God?

### SPOILER ALERT

ONE LAST STORY ABOUT Lena.

A few days after Christmas, we were in the deli line at the grocery store when a young dad turned from the two preschoolers in his care to strike up a conversation with my daughter, age three.

"Did Santa bring you something good this year?" he asked.

As you know, I grew up Jewish in a small town in Virginia. And, as you know, I'm fond of Christmas. When someone wishes me a "Merry Christmas," I typically respond with a hearty "And a Merry Christmas to you." But this felt different. Asking a random child about Santa Claus in Albany, New York, where Yom Kippur is a public school holiday, struck me as a bit careless.

Indeed, my daughter looked confused, even troubled. I was straining to think of a polite way to tell the guy he was a jerk when Lena did it for me.

Solemnly, she said, "Santa Claus is just pretend." He looked stricken and came closer, glancing back at his two little cart-riders. "Don't tell my kids, okay," he said to Lena. "They still think he's real." Lena nodded, accepting the burden of discretion.

I was so proud of her for speaking up, and then so sad that she was immediately asked to keep quiet. To be a nice girl, she was expected to hold her tongue. She was expected to hide the truth as she knew it and respect a lie that others had constructed. A pleasant, harmless lie, you might say. But a lie, nonetheless.


## FAKING IT


THE *NEW YORK TIMES* Freakonomics blog once asked readers whether they ever faked religious belief. Responses ranged from "yes, definitely, or I'd be out of a job," to "yes, of course, everyone does in some way," to "no way—I am who I am." That was about ten years before I wrote this book, so I decided recently to ask it myself, in private Facebook groups for atheists. Do any of them make a conscious effort to pass as religious? Do they ever find themselves holding their tongues?

I thought the fact that more and more Americans are unaffiliated with religion—the Pew Research Center estimated three in
ten, in December 2021, part of a steadily upward trend[1]—and that
the most ever have told pollsters that they don't believe in God—
according to Gallup, 17 percent in 2022[2]— would make atheists
less liable to pretend. But it doesn't seem like all that much has
changed in the past ten years or so.

People still fake religious belief—or hide their own nonbelief—
for all kinds of reasons: to get kids into a good school, get a job,
keep a job, quiet potential proselytizers, volunteer in a church-run
charity, attend AA meetings, or make parents happy.

Texas, and the South in general, were much invoked. Grandparents came up often:

"It would upset my grandfather so much and he's 102."

"My grandparents raised me so I'll just keep it quiet until
they're dead."

"I am vocal about it with everyone except for my grandmother.
She is old and very Catholic and also extremely vindictive/pet-
ty. She is also very, very wealthy."

The overriding theme was just . . . getting along with people.
One person wrote to the *Times*, "If you live somewhere with a dominant ideology that is different from yours, faking it is a way of life."

ॐ

Although the deli-line dad asked Lena not to tell his kids the truth
about Santa, he didn't actually stop her from calling over to them
and setting the record straight. She stopped herself. It wasn't even
conscious self-restraint. It wouldn't have occurred to her to tell
them because it wouldn't have occurred to her to do anything to

upset him or his kids or even me, who was always hounding my children to be considerate of others. Nothing was stopping her from telling the truth except wanting to get along with people.

The position she was in was deeply familiar to me as a nonbeliever. Just as Santa Claus is, in America at least, frequently a child's First Invisible Being Who Answers Prayers, not telling your peers the truth about Santa is often a child's First Self-Censorship for the Sake of Others. Whether it starts with Santa or not, many of us live entire lives suffused with self-censorship and misrepresentations that range from staying quiet to saying things we don't believe to going through the motions at church on Sunday. This is not a new phenomenon. The Greek philosopher Epicurus thought religious worship was a waste of time . . . except that "our happiness depends in part on living in peace with our fellow citizens."[3]

Ah, yes, living in peace. Like preschool Lena, I want to be a nice girl who never spoils anyone's fun. But I am an atheist in a world full of people who believe in God. Three-year-old Lena had an advantage over middle-aged me: her peers would eventually find out the truth on their own and the cognitive barrier between them—the wall of lies—would eventually fall. I don't have that moment to look forward to. There will always be grown-ups who believe, and saying "God is just pretend" to them just seems unnecessarily mean, like ripping off Santa's beard. At the very least, it seems rude. Daniel Dennett, in *Breaking the Spell*, likens speaking rationally about religious belief to letting one's cell phone ring in the middle of a concert. "How evil is it to break somebody's spell!"[4]

## OUR VEGAN COUSINS

WHY IS SAYING WHAT one believes such a disruptive act? I didn't ask my Facebook groups if they'd ever filed a lawsuit about "In God We Trust," protested the tax-exempt status of religious organizations, or tried to convince their neighbors not to believe. I asked only if they had always been honest about their true beliefs, and many of them responded as if I'd asked whether they had vandalized a church. Goodness, no!

Some people believe in God and some people don't. Most people who believe in God know that belief in God is not universal. It shouldn't come as a shock—but it is absolutely taken as an affront. Sort of like being a vegan.

A vegan is simply someone who intentionally forgoes the consumption of animals or animal products. That's it. One would think such a choice is of zero concern to anyone but the host of a dinner party. But vegans, as a group, are vilified to the extent that a (non-vegan) columnist wrote a piece titled "Stop Mocking Vegans"[5] and an article in *Vox* pondered, "Why do people hate vegans so much?"[6]

One study tried to figure it out.[7] Researchers surveyed omnivores and discovered they held views of vegans that were at least as negative as public perceptions of atheists and worse than homosexuals (to name just a couple of other common targets of widespread prejudice). But it seems the negativity wasn't so much in reaction to what vegans refused eat; people who swore off gluten didn't bother them as much. What people seemed to care about was *why* vegans ate what they did. Omnivores were especially negative toward vegans and vegetarians who were motivated by animal rights or environmental concerns rather than health. Eschewing meat-eating for political, philosophical, or moral reasons was what truly offended them. Weight loss? Fine. Morality? Fuck off.

Why? The study's authors speculate that, by abstaining from animal-based food for moral reasons, vegans "undermine the integrity of prevailing social values and traditions that exploit animals."

Undermining "prevailing social values and traditions"? As an atheist, I can relate. And people take that "undermining" stuff personally. The authors conclude that failing to "endorse mainstream ideologies and behaviors" threatens the status quo,[8] but it's more than that: it threatens how people think about themselves. Atheism and veganism

both exist as possible ways of living that fall outside of dominant social norms. The fact of them—the fact of us—throws into question
what most people believe to be true and normal and right.

No wonder we are widely disliked cultural minorities: our very
existence makes people feel bad about themselves. An atheist's existence says, "You have been duped"; a vegan's says, "You are com-
plicit." Feeling judged, people then preemptively judge others for
being judgmental, stereotyping vegans, for example, as insufferably
self-righteous and preachy. As the joke goes: *Q: How do you know
if someone's vegan? A: Don't worry, they'll tell you.* Vegans should
be preachy, in my opinion, given that they are taking the highly
unusual step of acting on their—scientifically sound and morally compelling—convictions. But I've never actually met a preachy
vegan—unless asking a waiter what's in the risotto counts as flaunt-
ing one's moral superiority.

The Preachy Vegan trope persists, nonetheless. It's cousin to the
Sneering Atheist, glimpsed here in this snippet of dialogue from
Plato's *Laws* (emphasis mine):

### CLINIAS

What, then, shall we do or say to [godless people]?

### ATHENIAN

Let us listen first, my good sir, to what they, as I imagine, say
*mockingly*, in their *contempt* for us.

### CLINIAS

What is it?

### ATHENIAN

In *derision* they would probably say this . . .[9]

Even before he puts words in the mouths of these hypothetical
godless people, we already know they are total assholes.

In real life—as opposed to in Plato's head—they probably wouldn't say anything because, as a respondent to the *New York Times* query put it, "I don't like telling people that everything they've ever believed is wrong."

## CONCEALABLE STIGMATIZED IDENTITIES (CSI'S)

ATHEISTS HAVE OTHER KIN at the reunion of social misfits, including the LGBTQ community. Like atheism, homosexuality is a difference that can be hidden. Sociologists call it a Concealable Stigmatized Identity, or CSI. A CSI could be anything about yourself that you want to hide and that can be hidden because, unlike race and age, it's not clearly perceptible from the outside. It could be depression or drug abuse or being a Republican in Brooklyn. People who aren't straight or cisgender lie about their sexual orientation or gender to protect themselves from discrimination and disinheritance scenes just as atheists do.

Clearly, there's a huge difference. LGBTQ people who are honest about their identities risk harassment, violence, and legal jeopardy. Atheists never had to fight for the right to marry or worry that their children might be beaten to death or bullied into suicide because of not believing in God. American atheists, that is. According to the most recent Humanists International Freedom of Thought report, eleven countries have blasphemy or apostasy laws that carry an ultimate penalty of death.[10] Others deny atheists the right to marry or to raise their children. In dozens more countries, persecution of atheists is less official, but still culturally accepted, widespread, and often violent.

American atheists don't typically face this kind of abuse. But we do face more than social disapproval or the risk of upsetting a father-in-law. Seven states clearly codify discrimination toward atheists in their constitutions. I'll quote just three.

**Maryland Declaration of Rights, Article 36**
That as it is the duty of every man to worship God in such manner as he thinks most acceptable to Him, all persons are equally entitled to protection in their religious liberty; . . . provided, he believes in the existence of God.

**Tennessee State Constitution, Article 9, Section 2**
No person who denies the being of God, or a future state of rewards and punishments, shall hold any office in the civil department of this state.

**North Carolina State Constitution, Article 6, Section 8**
The following persons shall be disqualified for office: First, any person who shall deny the being of Almighty God.

These clauses don't just *seem* unconstitutional, they have been ruled as such in 1961 in *Torcaso v. Watson*. So why haven't they been removed from the books? The Maryland state constitution has been amended 234 times since it was written. Surely, they could have removed the part about how you have to believe in God to sit on a jury. In 2022, Tennessee lawmakers voted to amend Article 9, Section 1, of their constitution, which states, "No minister of the Gospel, or priest of any denomination whatever, shall be eligible to a seat in either House of the Legislature." While they were cleaning things up, could they not also have taken a gander at Article 9, Section 2?

Todd Stiefel, chairman of the Openly Secular Coalition, told the *New York Times*, "If it was on the books that Jews couldn't hold public office, or that African-Americans or women couldn't vote, that would be a no-brainer. You'd have politicians falling all over themselves to try to get it repealed. Even if it was still unenforceable, it would still be disgraceful and be removed. So why are we different?"[11]

Apparently, the perceived political cost of being the legislator who champions the change is just too high. Politically speaking, atheism remains a huge liability. Pew Research Center surveyed Americans before the 2016 presidential election and found that being an atheist was the most negative possible trait, worse than being gay, old, adulterous, or completely lacking experience.[12] A 2020 Gallup poll found the percentage of people who said they were willing to vote for an atheist had gone up slightly, but atheists were still more likely than any group other than socialists to be excluded from a voter's consideration.[13]

In any case, we rarely get to put Americans' tolerance of atheism to the test; there's almost never an admitted atheist to vote for. To my knowledge, only one member of Congress has ever called himself an atheist—Californian Pete Stark, who served from 1973 to 2013. Representing California's second district, Congressman Jared Huffman calls himself a humanist, which is pretty close. But that's also pretty much it.

As far as we know. There could be others who are keeping it to themselves. After all, atheists as a group tend to believe that church and state should be kept separate and that one's religion or lack thereof should not be anyone else's business. They also tend to disapprove of the fact that religious people make a show of their faith in the public sphere (as one of my respondents said, "I don't shout it out like religious people do with their religions"). It makes sense, then, that atheists would be disinclined to put their metaphysical beliefs front and center—especially if it puts them at a political disadvantage. If you are serious about a political career, it's safer to keep your lack of belief to yourself. What would be the point of revealing a stigmatized identity that's easy to conceal?

That's a fair question for them. And it's a fair question for you, too.

My answer is: the point would be to erase the stigma.

Let's return to the LGBTQ community. In my lifetime, there has been a swift and seismic change in public opinion about sexual orientations other than straight and about genders other than cis. This cultural change is reflected in that same Gallup poll, which shows that in 1983 only 29 percent of Americans said they'd be willing to vote for a gay or lesbian candidate; in 2020 it was 78 percent. For atheists, approval has also grown, but far more slowly: from 42 percent of the public who, in 1983, were willing to vote for an atheist candidate to 60 percent in 2020.[14] Another Gallup poll shows that Americans' approval of same-sex marriage grew from 27 percent in 1996 to 71 percent in 2022.[15] That's an incredible change in public opinion over a relatively short time—a change caused at least in part by an intentional strategy of revealing stigmatized difference that might have been concealed.

Here's what Harvey Milk, one of the first openly gay elected officials in the United States, said in a speech in June 1978:

> You must come out. Come out . . . to your parents . . . I know that it is hard and will hurt them but think about how they will hurt you in the voting booth! Come out to your relatives . . . come out to your friends . . . if indeed they are your friends. Come out to your neighbors . . . to your fellow workers . . . to the people who work where you eat and shop . . . come out only to the people you know, and who know you. Not to anyone else. But once and for all, break down the myths, destroy the lies and distortions.[16]

It was easier for people to demonize and discriminate against homosexuals if they didn't know any—or didn't think they did. But once they found out their colleague's kid and their second cousin and their favorite comedian were gay, the mystery and the threat began to dwindle. Homosexuality, celebrity by celebrity, beloved aunt by favorite teacher, revelation by revelation, became just another variant of normal. As Alex Ross described it in "Love on the March,"

> In the end, the big change likely came about because, each year, a few thousand more gay people make the awkward an-

nouncement to their families and friends, supplanting images from the folklore of disgust.[17]

The people who heeded Milk's cry were taking an enormous risk, and Milk himself was assassinated just months later. But they gained so much—for others, if not for themselves. "Coming out" changed public opinion, and the law eventually, and imperfectly, followed, which helped change public opinion even more. The right to marry, the right to adopt, the right to serve in the military. Even the Boy Scouts ended its official ban.

Against gay people, that is. The organization still bans atheists. So let's say the same strategy of speaking out—of revealing one's Concealable Stigmatized Identity—will help reduce the bias against atheists in America. What's that really going to do for anyone other than a few future presidential candidates and Boy Scout troop leaders? Why make that awkward announcement if you don't have to? As one of my respondents said, "I just haven't seen a reason to 'out' myself."

I can give you two.

The first is to give others permission to live their lives more honestly. "Several times in the past 20 years," wrote someone in response to my Facebook question, "people have come out to me as the only atheist they know. So being open gives others the courage to do the same." Another person said, "Coming out" as an atheist could "help others feel safer and inspire some to stand with you." And my favorite: "My son came out about 10 years ago, so I borrowed from his strength and followed." You could be that person for your mother—or even for your 102-year-old grandfather. After all, we don't really know what's in people's heads. The woman who followed her son's example had thought she didn't know any other atheists, but "now I realize atheists are all around me."

When the writer Ali Rizvi was honest with his family about his lack of belief, a heated debate ensued. The next day he got an email from an adolescent nephew who had overheard it all: "Uncle Ali, I agree with your ideas and so do my friends. Please keep doing what you do and don't tell my parents I sent you this."[18]

It might not be instantaneous. It might be more like sowing than harvesting. But the more that atheists reveal the truth about themselves, the more that people in our lives can borrow from our strength, voice their own beliefs, be honest with their own loved ones, and be true to themselves. You could hardly give someone something more valuable than that.

The habit of intellectual honesty has, I believe, made my family closer than we would have been if we had never cast doubt on the essential veracity of our inherited religion or if we had simply gone through the motions. I'm sure there are subjects my kids feel uncomfortable discussing with me, but, I hope, there are far fewer than in families that lie about their religious beliefs (or avoid talking about sex, or pretend they never did drugs, or continue to honor family secrets). I have sown honesty and reaped trust—along with intellectual challenge, emotional sustenance, and joy.

My children have grown up with a keen sensor for distinguishing fact from fiction, but, far from turning them into "bloodless intellectual robot[s],"[19] as historian Susan Jacoby has described the cliché atheist, that power of perception has made their thinking richer and more layered, not less. They know bullshit when they hear it, but they also know great art when they experience it. Distinguishing what is real and what is fabricated has not led them to disparage the act of fabrication—far from it. We do not sit around as a family disdaining what was created by humans; we exalt it. My children are both enchanted by a great movie or song or story and curious about how it was made. They have become able critics and artists and cultural consumers and, not incidentally, engaged, informed, and savvy citizens.

Again: these are all gifts we could enjoy privately, no public revelation required. But being honest about what you believe in public is the only way to share those gifts beyond your family.

You can look at the question from the other side, too, if you respond better to guilt than to inspiration: continuing to conceal or misrepresent what you believe puts pressure on others to do the same. In "Passing: The Ethics of Pretending to Be What You Are Not," philosopher Claudia Mills writes, "The more we must package ourselves to fit a dominant social image, the more the dominance of that image is reinforced."[20] The more that good people pretend to believe in God, or let other people think they do, the more that people will think you have to believe in God to be good. The more that parents raise their children religiously out of habit, uncertainty, or fear rather than conviction, the more parents will think there's no other way to raise children. Everyone who conceals the truth makes it harder for other people to be honest.

## SAVE THE COUNTRY

WHICH BRINGS US TO the second reason to come out as an atheist: to save the country.

The presumption of belief has an effect not just on nonbelievers, but on every aspect of life in America. Let's take one example. In 2021, the House of Representatives passed the Equality Act, which would amend the 1964 Civil Rights Act so that it explicitly banned discrimination against people based on sexual orientation and gender identity in such realms as jobs, housing, education, and public accommodation. Under the Equality Act, businesses couldn't refuse to serve someone because of their sexual orientation or gender identity, just as they cannot on account of race. Fair enough. But the Equality Act has been described as a controversial measure and is unlikely to pass the Senate and become law. Why? "Religious freedom." Since the law specifically limits the ability of people to claim their religious beliefs allow them to discriminate against others, it would, according to a joint statement of Catholic bishops, "discriminate against people of faith."[21] The Coalition for Jewish Values calls the Equality Act "a disgraceful attack upon Jewish Biblical beliefs."[22]

Atheists are not subject to anything like the prejudice that LGBTQ people face. It's not even close. But peel back the layers of discrimination against LGBTQ people and you find religion. Peel back layers of control over women's bodies—from dress codes that punish girls for male desire all the way to the Supreme Court striking down *Roe v. Wade*—and you find religion. "Our creator endowed us with the right to life" was how Governor Greg Abbott of Texas explained his state's extreme restrictions on abortion. Peel back the layers of abstinence-only or marriage-centered or anti-homosexual sex education and you find religion. "Don't Say Gay" laws, school-library book bans, and even the backlash against acknowledging the racist underpinnings of our nation are motivated by religion.

If you start to look, religion is at the center of every battle against scientific and social progress. And when it loses a fight and progress wins instead, religion then claims it's not subject to the laws that result. "Religious belief" is—more and more, both at the state and federal level—a way to sidestep every advance the country makes in terms of civil rights, human rights, and public health. In some places, pharmacists can refuse to fill prescriptions based on religious belief, elected officials can refuse to do their jobs based on religious belief, and businesses can refuse certain customers based on religious belief. Catholic hospitals that receive public funds can refuse to perform sterilizations, abortions, even end-of-life care. Businesses with federal contracts can claim religious belief when fighting claims of discrimination. Nine out of ten states permit religious exemptions from laws that require children who attend school to be vaccinated. When other public venues had to shut down or curb their occupancy during the pandemic, many places of worship got a pass. Meanwhile, the protections of the Establishment Clause are beginning to weaken: the Supreme Court has ruled that the citizens of Maine have to pay for parochial school and that a high school football coach should be free to lead a prayer on the fifty-yard line.

You don't have to hate religion or feel disdain toward religious people to think that religious belief should not be shaping public policy. Or to see that the prejudices written into the foundational myths of the world's three major monotheistic religions are driving much of the discrimination our fellow Americans suffer today.

If you pretend to believe when you really don't, you allow people to behave as if belief in the supernatural is universal. As if it's not just the norm, but the only belief that is or should be normal. As if "God's will" has any place in a discussion of public policy. These belief systems don't just make it risky to be honest to American voters. They elevate the value of religion and religious belief over public health, scientific inquiry, civil rights, and economic justice.

So, no, anti-atheist sentiment is not a matter of life and death in America. But transphobia is, sexual violence against women is, forced birth is, climate change is, and global pandemics are. If you need a reason to let people know that you don't believe moral authority derives from a Supreme Being, then I offer you no less than making America a safer, smarter, more just, and more compassionate country.

ᥰ·

I wasn't thinking about these issues when I first made the decision to be honest about being an atheist. The political situation was dire even then, but it's gotten far, far scarier with the growing power of the religious right, the tilt of the Supreme Court, the eruption of Christian nationalist violence, and the well-established connection between fundamentalism and disinformation.[23] The ground the LGBTQ community so quickly gained now suddenly seems shaky.

I like to think that if I were deciding now, in the current political climate, I would be quicker to call myself an atheist, if for no other reason than to rebuke those who attempt to use "God" to control other people's lives. And to rebuke those who let them. I like to imagine myself quickly relinquishing the comfortable label of Jew in favor of the more pointed, more honest "atheist." But back then, I hesitated. Maybe I was just too young. Many people who responded to my internet query spoke of "passing" as if that were a specific period in their lives. "I was a poser for a time." "I am past that stage now." "I've outgrown the need to do that."

Well, I was a poser, too, a passer, a nice, chatty mom with an embarrassing CSI. I was, in short, exactly the sort of person who needed to come out.

If "atheist" is ever going to stop being a scary word—and if "religious" is ever going to stop being a sacred word, a word that short-circuits moral and scientific progress—atheists have to be willing to say in casual conversation that we are atheists. Not just the full-time activists among us, the evolutionary biologists, the celebrity comedians. All of us.

## THE COMBINATION FORM

OF COURSE, YOU CAN call yourself a humanist or an agnostic, you can call yourself lapsed or nonobserving or unaffiliated or "spiritual but not religious." "Free thinker"—fine. But if you don't believe that there is a supernatural being in charge of the universe, then I strongly recommend that you call yourself an atheist, both to defang the word and to clarify the point.

That, I concede, is a lot to ask if your faith tradition is part of your identity. For many people, the religion they grew up in is part of who they are. And for those of us who belong to a minority faith community, failing to claim it can feel like a betrayal. Do you have to give up one part of your identity—the way you were raised—in order to claim another—the way you think?

In *The Lies That Bind*, Kwame Anthony Appiah argues that religious belief and religious identity are separate things and can be treated as such.

> Amartya Sen, the great Indian economist and philosopher, once told me how, as a child, he went to ask his grandfather about Hinduism. You're too young, he was told, come back when you're older. So he came back as a teenager to try again. But he had to begin by warning his grandfather that he had decided in the interim that he didn't believe in the gods. There you are, his grandfather replied, you belong to the atheist branch of the Hindu tradition.[24]

Appiah describes the fluidity of religious practice, the way you can engage in the practices of one belief system (say, pour out libations to one's ancestors as do the Asante people of Ghana) while professing the beliefs of another (say, Islam or Christianity).[25] We are not always one thing or another, even religiously. Nor have we been in millennia past. As Christianity began to flourish in the fourth, fifth, and sixth centuries, writes Tim Whitmarsh in *Battling the Gods*, "polytheism and Christianity could exist side by side without any obvious friction." In fact, it was "easy to be a Christian and something else."[26]

Many of the atheists I know are atheists and something else. I am. There are absolutely situations in which I feel like the correct thing to do—not doctrinally but politically and even emotionally—is to name myself a Jew, even though I don't believe in Judaism. "Atheist" expresses how I think about the world. "Jewish" expresses how I was raised and with whom I learned to identify.

So what if instead of jettisoning the label you've used your whole life, you just add to it? If you don't want to abandon the religio-cultural heritage of your youth, may I suggest a combination form? You could be a Jewish atheist, an Irish-Catholic atheist, or a Muslim atheist. If your Minnesota upbringing is dear to you, you could be a Lutheran atheist. Raised in a Black church in Alabama? "AME atheist" has a nice ring to it.

Those combinations may seem paradoxical, but that doesn't make them untrue. And if they strike you as heretical, the nice thing is that you don't believe in the God who would be offended.

## EASY FOR ME TO SAY

OVER THE YEARS, I gradually learned to be honest about not believing in God, and once or twice that honesty put me in true conflict with others. But my struggle was mostly with myself: my own need to be liked, my own blurry thinking, my own uncertainty. The drama outside my head was relatively minor. My husband and I are metaphysically in sync. My family and friends are fine with my being an atheist. My community is filled with churches, mosques, and synagogues, but it also has a humanist society. The evangelical Christian polling firm Barna Group determined that the Albany metropolitan area is the sixth-most post-Christian city in America.[27] I'm not sure what that means, but I assume it's a badge of honor, like when the NRA gives you an F. As a white person, I face far less pressure to conceal my identity than do Black nonbelievers.[28] Also, and I think this is important to note: I was able to have it both ways. It's relatively common for Jews to use that combination form, since Jewish identity is already somewhat uncoupled from the Jewish belief system. I can call myself an atheist and a Jew if I want, and sometimes I do.

In short, I didn't risk much when I took my turn toward the truth. Sam Harris tells a story in *Lying* about reentering the country from Asia and answering "yes" when a US Customs officer asked whether he took any drugs while he was there. They had a conversation about opium while the man searched his bag. He concludes,

"One thing was perfectly clear at the end of our encounter: We both felt very good about it."[29] Although Harris acknowledges it might have been different if he had been trying to smuggle drugs, he doesn't acknowledge how helpful it was to be a white male of means—in this anecdote in particular or in his freedom in general to prioritize truth telling over, say, conciliation. I've been thinking about privilege a lot recently in terms of my own determination to be honest with the world around me. I didn't face the barriers or risks that others do, and I've suffered little for the rewards that I've reaped. It caused a bit of extended-family drama. It may have cost my husband some votes. I am not universally beloved on Twitter or in *Washington Post* comment threads, which of course I otherwise would be. But that's it, and it's not much.

I fully concede this point. In fact, I insist on it. Because there are a lot of concealed atheists for whom, as for me, the rewards of honesty are high and the costs are low. We who risk little have, I believe, an even greater responsibility to be honest and outspoken. There are people in this country, and in the world at large, for whom the consequences of admitting to their nonbelief are grave. For their sake, for the sake of those who must continue to conceal, I believe those who don't have to keep quiet should speak up. Rizvi writes that he and his like-minded friends have a special responsibility as atheist Muslims living in societies where free speech is a right. "We speak out as often as we can for all those back home who can't."[30]

᪥

When I was finishing this book, I called up Rebecca Vitsmun, the Oklahoma tornado survivor who told Wolf Blitzer that, no, in fact, she did not thank God for her survival because she was "actually an atheist." I wanted to know what had happened after she made her nationally televised revelation. I knew she had hidden her atheism from her parents and her colleagues up until then. Did she suffer any consequence from telling the truth?

The answer was no. Vitsmun was thirty when the tornado hit; she said she had known since she was nineteen that she was an atheist, but she hadn't told her parents because "it just felt easier not to." Her family was quite religious; she was raised Catholic but her family included a Baptist speaker and an Episcopalian pastor. Before she identified herself as an atheist, her mother would ask occasionally if she was going to church and she would lightly laugh it off—"No, of course not." She never came out and said anything specific because she didn't want to hurt anyone's feelings or cause a scene. Or just make life harder.

But it turns out, it didn't make life harder. When her mom found out, she first tried to convince Vitsmun she wasn't an atheist because she believed in a higher power ("Mom," Vitsmun replied, "I wouldn't have said atheist if that was the case"), and then she said to her daughter, "I know you're a good person."

Some people started praying for Vitsmun, and some people she didn't particularly want to talk to stopped talking to her. People who disagreed with her kept their distance—"I've never run into anybody who gave me any type of grief," she said, even when she wears atheist T-shirts in deep-red states. But she did, and still does, get approached by people who are relieved and grateful that she made herself be honest on television. Or by people who had been thinking about these things but had no one to talk to. Or by people who want to tell her that they "pulled a Rebecca Vitsmun" because, say, at the doctor's office, they corrected the assumption of belief.

You could do that too.

If you think you'd lose your job or put your children at risk of harassment, you get a pass. If you would be risking physical harm, don't speak out. If you're an atheist running for school board on the buckle of the Bible Belt, then feel free to keep it quiet, and God bless.

But if you're just trying to avoid your dad's disapproval or an awkward conversation at the PTA membership table, if you just can't stand the thought that someone might not like you, please consider taking a deep breath and coming out with the truth.

# NOTES

## PROLOGUE: ACTUALLY AN ATHEIST

1  TED Radio Hour, "Sandi Toksvig: Can Social Change Start with Laughter?" NPR, March 24, 2017.
2  Gregory A. Smith, "About Three-in-Ten U.S. Adults Are Now Religiously Unaffiliated," Pew Research Center's Religion & Public Life Project, December 14, 2021.
3  Smith, "About Three-in-Ten."
4  Lydia Saad and Zach Hrynowski, "How Many Americans Believe in God?" Gallup.com, June 24, 2022.
5  Lydia Saad, "Socialism and Atheism Still U.S. Political Liabilities," Gallup.com, February 11, 2020.
6  Michael Lipka and Jessica Martínez, "So, You Married an Atheist . . . ." Pew Research Center, June 16, 2014.
7  Will M. Gervais and Maxine Belén Najle, "How Many Atheists Are There?" PsyArXiv, January 23, 2017.
8  Daniel C. Dennett, *Breaking the Spell* (New York and London: Penguin, 2007), 56.
9  Rebecca Vitsmun, interview with TheThinkingAtheist, November 2, 2013.

## PART ONE: THE MAKING OF AN ATHEIST

### SHENANDOAH VALLEY JEW

1  *The Holy Bible: New Revised Standard Version* (New York: Oxford University Press, 1989). All subsequent citations of the Bible refer to this edition.

### PASSING

1  Kate Cohen, *The Neppi Modona Diaries* (Hanover, NH: UPNE, 1997), 157.

## THUNDERBOLT
1    Ingri and Edgar Parin D'Aulaire, *Ingri and Edgar Parin d'Aulaire's Book of Greek Myths* (Garden City, NY: Doubleday Books for Young Readers, 1962), 9.

## THE TRUTH, THE PARTIAL TRUTH, AND NOTHING LIKE THE TRUTH
1    Sam Harris, *Lying* (Opelousas, LA: Four Elephants Press, 2013), 5.

## WHY I DON'T CALL MYSELF AN AGNOSTIC
1    Tim Whitmarsh, *Battling the Gods* (New York: Alfred A. Knopf, 2015), 59.
2    Dennett, *Breaking the Spell*, 209.

## SORRY, HONEY, GOD'S JUST PRETEND
1    Paul-Henri Thiry (Baron d'Holbach), *Good Sense without God*, trans. unlisted (London: W. Stewart & Co., 1900), section 35, Kindle.
2    Kathleen H. Corriveau, Eva E. Chen, and Paul L. Harris, "Judgments about Fact and Fiction by Children from Religious and Nonreligious Backgrounds," *Cognitive Science* 39, no. 2 (March 2015): 353–82.
3    Jane Wynne Willson, *Parenting without God* (Nottingham, UK: Educational Heretics Press, 1997), 50–51.
4    Wendy Thomas Russell, *Relax, It's Just God* (Long Beach, CA: Brown Paper Press, 2015), 44.
5    Deborah Mitchell, *Growing Up Godless* (New York: Sterling Ethos, 2014), 192.
6    Dennett, *Breaking the Spell*, 86.

## HUBRIS
1    Saad and Hrynowski, "How Many."
2    Megan Brenan, "40% of Americans Believe in Creationism," Gallup.com, July 26, 2019.
3    Gregory A. Smith, "Few Americans Blame God or Say Faith Has Been Shaken Amid Pandemic, Other Tragedies," Pew Research Center's Religion & Public Life Project, December 14, 2021.
4    Ovid, "The Metamorphoses," trans. A. S. Kline (The Ovid Collection, University of Virginia, 2000), bk. VIII.
5    Ovid, "The Metamorphoses," bk. VI.
6    Ovid, "The Metamorphoses," bk. VI.
7    Whitmarsh, *Battling the Gods*, 47.
8    Seyyed Hossein Nasr, ed., *The Study Quran* (San Francisco: HarperOne, 2015). All subsequent citations of the Quran refer to this edition.

9    C. S. Lewis, *Mere Christianity* (San Francisco: HarperOne, 2001), 122.

10   Joseph Delany, "Pride," *The Catholic Encyclopedia* (New York: Robert Appleton Company, 1911), vol. 12.

11   Quoted in Whitmarsh, *Battling the Gods*, 170.

12   Whitmarsh, *Battling the Gods*, 159.

13   Moses Maimonides, *Guide for the Perplexed*, trans. M. Friedlander (London: Routledge and Keegan Paul Ltd., 1904) 2:29:27.

14   Ali A. Rizvi, *The Atheist Muslim* (New York: St. Martin's Press, 2016), 109.

15   Rizvi, *The Atheist Muslim*, 110.

16   Rizvi, *The Atheist Muslim*, 112.

17   Wendy Beckett, *Sister Wendy on Prayer* (New York: Harmony, 2010), 117.

18   Sasha Sagan, *For Small Creatures Such as We* (New York: G. P. Putnam's Sons, 2019), 10.

19   Phil Zuckerman, *Society without God* (New York: NYU Press, 2010), 155.

20   Rodney Stark and Roger Finke, *Acts of Faith* (Berkeley and Los Angeles: University of California Press, 2000), 85.

## PART TWO: WHAT WE LOSE AND WHAT WE GAIN

### LIFE WITH NO AFTER

1    Todd May, *Death* (London: Routledge, 2014), 4.

2    Pascal Boyer, *Religion Explained* (New York: Basic Books, 2007), 204.

3    Karen Armstrong, *A Short History of Myth* (Edinburgh: Canongate Books, 2005), 3, 1.

4    Lewis Black, *Me of Little Faith* (New York and London: Riverhead Books, 2008), 14.

5    Leo Tolstoy, *The Death of Ivan Ilych*, trans. Louise and Aylmer Maude (West Jordan City, UT: Waking Lion Press, 2006), 8, 9.

6    Tolstoy, *The Death of Ivan Ilych*, 49.

7    Uniform Law Commission, "Determination of Death Act," 1980.

8    May, *Death*, 12.

9    May, *Death*, 14.

10   Rizvi, *The Atheist Muslim*, 60.

11   May, *Death*, 4.

12   Timothy Keller, *On Death* (New York: Penguin, 2020), 33.

13   Keller, *On Death*, 19.

14   William Shakespeare, *Hamlet*, in *The Complete Works* (New York: Penguin Books, 1969), Act 5, scene 1, 193.

15   Tolstoy, *The Death of Ivan Ilych*, 50.

16   Sagan, *For Small Creatures*, 67.

17 Epicurus, "Letter to Menoeceus," in *The Essential Epicurus*, trans. Eugene O'Connor (Buffalo, NY: Great Books in Philosophy, 1993), 63.
18 Epicurus, *Essential*, 63.
19 Kieran Setiya, *Midlife: A Philosophical Guide* (Princeton, NJ: Princeton University Press, 2017), 108.
20 Setiya, *Midlife*, 108.
21 Epicurus, *Essential*, 64.
22 Setiya, *Midlife*, 154.

## HOW TO START YOUR OWN HOLIDAY

1 Josef Pieper, *In Tune with the World*, trans. Richard and Clara Winston (South Bend, IN: St Augustine Press, 1999), 24.
2 Pieper, *In Tune*, 34.
3 Pieper, *In Tune*, 58.
4 Pieper, *In Tune*, 41, 39.
5 Pieper, *In Tune*, 34.
6 Sagan, *For Small Creatures*, 197.
7 Nancy F. Castaldo, *Pizza for the Queen* (New York: Holiday House, 2005).
8 Gregory I, "Letter to Abbot Mellitus" (internet Medieval Sourcebook), Epistola 76, PL 77: 1215–16.
9 Sagan, *For Small Creatures*, 16.
10 Pieper, *In Tune*, 27.
11 Pieper, *In Tune*, 19.
12 Pieper, *In Tune*, 18.
13 Pieper, *In Tune*, 24.

## HOW WILL WE KNOW RIGHT FROM WRONG?

1 Dennett, *Breaking the Spell*, 249.
2 Maryland Declaration of Rights, Article 36.
3 Pennsylvania State Constitution, Article 1, Section 4. Tennessee says the same thing in the negative—you can't hold office if you don't believe that you will be punished for your sins one day. Tennessee State Constitution, Article 9, Section 2.
4 In *Torcaso v. Watkins* (1961) the Supreme Court found that the state's requirement of belief in God violated the First and Fourteenth Amendments of the US Constitution, so the legislature amended Article 36 of Maryland's constitution in 1970. Instead of removing the unconstitutional religious test, they just added the sentence, "Nothing in this article shall constitute an establishment of religion."
5 Christine Tamir, Aidan Connaughton, and Ariana Monique Salazar, "The Global God Divide," Pew Research Center's Global Attitudes Project, July 20, 2020.

6   William Barr, "Remarks to The Law School and The De Nicola Center For Ethics And Culture." United States Department of Justice, October 11, 2019.

7   Mike Cason, "Candidate Dean Young Says Alabama Gov. Kay Ivey Lied About Ten Commandments Commitment," AL.com, May 24, 2022.

8   168 Cong. Rec. H5385 (daily ed. June 8, 2022) (statement of Rep. Steube).

9   Alex Haley, "Interview with Rev. Martin Luther King," *Playboy*, January 1965.

10  Will M. Gervais, Dimitri Xygalatas, et al., "Global Evidence of Extreme Intuitive Moral Prejudice against Atheists," Nature Human Behavior 1, no. 8 (August 7, 2017).

11  Hemant Mehta, "In 2021, Atheists Made Up Only 0.1% of the Federal Prison Population." OnlySky Media, February 28, 2022.

12  Kwame Anthony Appiah, *The Lies That Bind* (New York: Liveright Publishing, 2018), 59.

13  Barbara Ehrenreich, "The Missionary Position," *The Baffler*, November 2012.

14  Maureen Dowd, "Why, God?" *The New York Times*, December 25, 2012.

15  David Hume, *Dialogues Concerning Natural Religion* (Project Gutenberg, 2009), part 10.

16  Epstein, *Good without God*, 33.

17  Anne Lamott, *Help, Thanks, Wow* (New York: Penguin, 2012), 84.

18  Rick Rojas, "A Church, a Gathering Place for Generations, Becomes a Hub for Uvalde's Grief," *The New York Times*, May 30, 2022.

19  "Sen. Myrdal on Her Bill Regarding the Ten Commandments," News & Views with Joel Heitkamp, February 5, 2021.

20  Parliament of the World's Religions. "Towards a Global Ethic: An Initial Declaration," 2016, 2.

21  Sahih Muslim 45, quoted in Yahya ibn Sharaf al-Nawawi, *The 40 Hadith of Imam Al-Nawawi*, ed. Sheik Akbar (Kindle, 2020), 21.

22  Bahá'u'lláh, *Tablets of Bahá'u'lláh Revealed After The Kitáb-i-Aqdas* (US Bahá'í Publishing Trust, 1988), 64.

23  Sutrakritanga 1.11.33, in Friedrich Max Müller, ed., *Jaina Sutras, Part II*, trans. Hermann Jacobi (Kindle, 2010), 347.

24  Confucius, *The Analects*, trans. Simon Leys (Oxford: Oxford Paperbacks, 2008), XII:2.

25  Oyekan Owomoyela, *Yoruba Proverbs* (Lincoln: Univ. of Nebraska Press, 2008), Kindle loc. 4363.

26  Fyodor Dostoevsky, *The Brothers Karamazov*, trans. Andrew R. MacAndrew (New York: Bantam Classics, 2011), 788.

27  Quoted in Whitmarsh, *Battling the Gods*, 95.

28   Rick Warren, *The Purpose-Driven Life* (Grand Rapids, MI: Zondervan, 2003), 52–53.

## TAKE ME TO CHURCH

1   Alain de Botton, *Religion for Atheists* (New York: Pantheon, 2012), 257.
2   De Botton, *The Architecture of Happiness* (New York: Vintage, 2008), 107.
3   De Botton, *Architecture*, loc. 227.
4   De Botton, *Architecture*, loc. 832.
5   Leon Battista Alberti, *On the Art of Building in Ten Books*, trans. Joseph Rykwert, Neil Leach, and Robert Tavernor (Cambridge: MIT Press, 1991), 229.
6   Alberti, *Art of Building*, 194.
7   De Botton, *Architecture*, loc. 863.
8   Episcopal Diocese of Albany, "Canon XVI – Marriage" (Accessed October 2, 2022).
9   De Botton, *Religion for Atheists*, 257.
10   De Botton, *Religion for Atheists*, 261 and 264.
11   De Botton, *Religion for Atheists*, 284.
12   George M. Spencer, "True Believers," *Dartmouth Alumni Magazine*, January 2019.
13   Casper ter Kuile, *The Power of Ritual* (New York: HarperCollins, 2020), 5.
14   Tara Isabella Burton, *Strange Rites* (New York: PublicAffairs, 2020), 7, 93.
15   Molly Phinney Baskette, *Real Good Church* (Cleveland, OH: Pilgrim Press, 2014), 51.
16   De Botton, *Architecture*, loc. 835.

## ARE YOU THERE, NOT ME? IT'S ME

1   *Gates of Prayer* (New York: Central Conference of American Rabbis, 1975; 1982), 445.
2   Vatican II Council, Constitution on the Sacred Liturgy *Sacrosanctum Consilium*, December 4, 1963, chapter 1, part 11.
3   *Town of Greece v. Galloway*, 572 US 565, 565 (2014).
4   *Joyner v. Forsyth County, NC, 653 F.3d 341, 347 (4th Cir. 2011)*.
5   *Joyner v. Forsyth County*.
6   *Town of Greece v. Galloway*.
7   Amanda Gorman, *The Hill We Climb* (New York: Viking, 2021), 29.
8   C. S. Lewis, *Letters to Malcolm: Chiefly on Prayer* (New York: Harcourt, Brace & World), 11.
9   Pete Holmes, *Dirty Clean* (HBO, 2018), minute 43.
10   Lewis, *Letters*, 77.

11    James Martin, *Learning to Pray* (San Francisco: HarperOne, 2021), 58.
12    Mary DeTurris Poust, *The Essential Guide to Catholic Prayer and the Mass* (New York: Alpha Books, 2011), 14.
13    Martin, *Learning to Pray*, 45.
14    Anne Lamott, *Help, Thanks, Wow*, 4.
15    Beckett, *Sister Wendy on Prayer*, 50.
16    Martin, *Learning to Pray*, 16.
17    Martin, *Learning to Pray*, 37–40.
18    Beckett, *Sister Wendy on Prayer*, 87.
19    Martin, *Learning to Pray*, 23.
20    Mark Twain, *The Adventures of Huckleberry Finn* (New York: Vintage Classics, 2010), 13-14.
21    Lewis, *Letters*, 58.
22    Emo Philips, "The Best God Joke Ever—And It's Mine," *The Guardian*, September 29, 2005.
23    Martin, *Learning to Pray*, 111.
24    Beckett, *Sister Wendy on Prayer*, 60.
25    Lewis, *Letters to Malcolm*, 60.
26    Piercarlo Valdesolo, "Scientists Find One Source of Prayer's Power," *Scientific American*, December 24, 2013.
27    Martin, *Learning to Pray*, 227.
28    Martin, 229.
29    Lamott, *Help, Thanks, Wow*, 2, 3.
30    Lamott, *Help, Thanks, Wow*, 32.
31    Lewis, *Letters to Malcolm*, 20.
32    Lewis, *Letters to Malcolm*, 21.
33    Beckett, *Sister Wendy on Prayer*, 103.
34    Lewis, *Letters to Malcom*, 22.
35    Shakespeare, *Hamlet*, Act III, scene iii, 57–64.
36    Shakespeare, *Hamlet*, Act III, scene iii, 97.
37    Beckett, *Sister Wendy on Prayer*, 39.
38    Andrew W. K., "Ask Andrew W. K.: Prayer Is Stupid, Right?" *The Village Voice*, September 3, 2014.
39    Sagan, *For Small Creatures*, 41.
40    Lewis, *Letters to Malcolm*, 113.

## RITE OF PASSAGE

1    Arnold van Gennep, *The Rites of Passage*, 2nd ed., trans. Monika B. Vizedom and Gabrielle L. Caffee (Chicago: University of Chicago Press, 2019), 71.
2    Van Gennep, *The Rites of Passage*, 71.
3    Zuckerman, *Society without God*, 161.
4    Zuckerman, *Society without God*, 154.

5   "Survey: Most Norwegians Do Not Believe in God," Nationen.no, June 26, 2022.
6   "Church of Norway," Statistics Norway, June 15, 2022.
7   "Confirmation," Church of Norway (kirken.no), accessed October 7, 2022.
8   Zuckerman, *Society without God*, 154.
9   Van Gennep, *The Rites of Passage*, 134.
10  Sextus Empiricus, *Selections from the Major Writings on Scepticism, Man, & God*, edited by Philip P. Hallie and trans. Sanford G. Etheridge (Indianapolis, IN: Hackett Publishing, 1985), 188.
11  Leo Tolstoy, *Anna Karenina*, trans. Louise and Aylmer Maude (New York: Everyman's Library, 1992), 517.
12  Tolstoy, *Anna Karenina*, 521.
13  Appiah, *The Lies That Bind*, 36.
14  Kate Cohen, *A Walk Down the Aisle: Notes on a Modern Wedding* (New York: W. W. Norton, 2001), 142.
15  Zuckerman, *Society without God*, 162.
16  Zuckerman, *Society without God*, 164.
17  Zuckerman, *Society without God*, 166.
18  "Baruch Sheptarani," *Bereshit Rabbah* 63:10 (Sefaria.com).
19  Jewish Virtual Library, "The 613 Mitzvot (Commandments)."
20  Van Gennep, *The Rites of Passage*, 176.
21  Van Gennep, *The Rites of Passage*, 178.

## UNPLUGGING FROM THE HIGHER POWER

1   Lamott, *Help, Thanks, Wow*, 99.
2   Brian Manzullo, "Dan Gilbert After Cavaliers Win: 'God Loves Cleveland, Ohio,'" *Detroit Free Press*, June 20, 2016.
3   Jim Denison, "Simone Biles Sees God's Hand in Her Successes and Her Disappointments," *Christian Parenting*, August 3, 2021.
4   Sarah C. Murray, "The Role of Religion in Greek Sport." In *A Companion to Sport and Spectacle in Greek and Roman Antiquity*, ed. Paul Christesen and Donald G. Kyle (John Wiley & Sons, 2013), 314.
5   Murray, "Role of Religion," 315.
6   Pindar, Olympian Ode VII, *The Extant Odes of Pindar*, trans. Ernest Myers (London: Macmillan and Co., 1874), Project Gutenberg.
7   Murray, "Role of Religion," 313.
8   Michael Morris, "US Divers on Qualifying for Olympics: 'We Can't Take Credit for This: To God Be the Glory.'" CNSNews.com, July 7, 2016.
9   Lisa Miller, "Pitching God," *New York Magazine*, June 17, 2013.
10  Murray, "Role of Religion," 312.
11  Ron Shelton, *Bull Durham* (Orion Pictures, 1988).

12   "ESPN Reporter Criticized for Reaction to Durant's Response to Interview Question," KFOR.com Oklahoma City, January 31, 2014.

13   Brandon Stanton, *Humans of New York: Stories* (London: Macmillan, 2015), 91.

14   Corinne Segal, "How a 'Humans of New York' Blog Post Inspired a Principal and a $1.2 Million Fundraiser," *PBS NewsHour*, February 5, 2015.

15   *Against the Rules*, Season 3, Episode 2: "The Art of the Untold Story," April 5, 2022.

16   Zuckerman, *Society without God*, 100.

17   Phil Zuckerman, "Secular Societies Fare Better Than Religious Societies," *Psychology Today*, October 13, 2014.

18   Zuckerman, *Society without God*, 18.

19   Melissa Alonso, "10-Year-Old Amerie Jo Garza Identified by Her Father as Victim in Uvalde Shooting," CNN, May 25, 2022.

20   *Alcoholics Anonymous Big Book* (Twelve Steps: The Companion app), 46.

## EPILOGUE: COMING OUT WITH THE TRUTH

1   Smith, "About Three-in-Ten."

2   Jeffrey M. Jones, "Belief in God in US Dips to 81%, a New Low," Gallup.com, June 17, 2022.

3   Quoted in Whitmarsh, *Battling the Gods*, 177.

4   Dennett, *Breaking the Spell*, 13.

5   Farhad Manjoo, "Stop Mocking Vegans." *The New York Times*, August 28, 2019.

6   Abigail Higgins, "Why Do People Hate Vegans So Much?" *Vox.com*, November 2, 2018.

7   Cara C. MacInnis and Gordon Hodson, "It ain't easy eating greens: Evidence of bias toward vegetarians and vegans from both source and target," *Journal of Group Processes and Intergroup Relations* 20, no. 6 (November 2017).

8   MacInnis and Hodson, "It ain't easy."

9   Plato, *Plato in Twelve Volumes*, vol. 11, trans. R. G. Bury (Cambridge: Harvard University Press, 1967) Book X:885c.

10   Humanists International, "Freedom of Thought Report," accessed October 5, 2022.

11   Laurie Goodstein, "In Seven States, Atheists Push to End Largely Forgotten Ban," *The New York Times*, December 6, 2014.

12   "For 2016 Hopefuls, Washington Experience Could Do More Harm Than Good," Pew Research Center, May 19, 2014.

13   Saad, "Socialism and Atheism."

14   Saad, "Socialism and Atheism."

15　Justin McCarthy, "Same-Sex Marriage Support Inches Up to New High Of 71%," Gallup.com, June 1, 2022.

16　Harvey Milk, "That's What America Is." Presented at the San Francisco Gay Freedom Day Parade, June 25, 1978.

17　Alex Ross, "Love on the March," *The New Yorker*, November 4, 2012.

18　Rizvi, *The Atheist Muslim*, 203.

19　Susan Jacoby, "The Blessings of Atheism," *The New York Times*, January 5, 2013.

20　Claudia Mills, "Passing: The Ethics of Pretending to Be What You Are Not," *Social Theory and Practice*, vol. 25, no. 1 (1999): 29–51.

21　United States Conference of Catholic Bishops, "US Bishop Chairmen Say Equality Act Would Discriminate Against People Of Faith And Threaten Unborn Life," February 3, 2021, accessed October 7, 2022.

22　"Equality Act Calls Bible a Bigoted Document, Says Rabbinic Group," Religion News Service, February 25, 2021.

23　Tom Jacobs, "Fundamentalists Are More Likely to Fall For Fake News," *Pacific Standard*, February 21, 2019.

24　Appiah, *The Lies That Bind*, 36.

25　Appiah, *The Lies That Bind*, 65

26　Whitmarsh, *Battling the Gods*, 234.

27　"The Most Post-Christian Cities in America: 2019," Barna Group, June 5, 2019.

28　American Atheists, "Black Atheists Often Feel Forced to Hide Their Beliefs, Resulting in Significant Harm, New Research Finds," Atheists.org, October 5, 2021.

29　Harris, *Lying*, 32.

30　Rizvi, *The Atheist Muslim*, 134.

# SELECTED BIBLIOGRAPHY

Alberti, Leon Battista. *On the Art of Building in Ten Books.* Translated by Joseph Rykwert, Neil Leach, and Robert Tavernor. Cambridge: MIT Press, 1991.

Appiah, Kwame Anthony. *The Lies That Bind: Rethinking Identity.* New York: Liveright Publishing, 2018.

Baskette, Molly Phinney. *Real Good Church: How Our Church Came Back from the Dead, and Yours Can, Too.* Cleveland, OH: Pilgrim Press, 2014.

Beckett, Wendy. *Sister Wendy on Prayer.* New York: Harmony, 2010.

Black, Lewis. *Me of Little Faith.* New York and London: Riverhead Books, 2008.

Boyer, Pascal. *Religion Explained: The Evolutionary Origins of Religious Thought.* New York: Basic Books, 2007.

Burton, Tara Isabella. *Strange Rites: New Religions for a Godless World.* New York: PublicAffairs, 2020.

Castaldo, Nancy F. *Pizza for the Queen.* New York: Holiday House, 2005.

Cohen, Kate. *A Walk Down the Aisle: Notes on a Modern Wedding.* New York: W. W. Norton, 2001.

———. *The Neppi Modona Diaries: Reading Jewish Survival through My Italian Family.* Hanover, NH: UPNE, 1997.

D'Aulaire, Ingri, and Edgar Parin D'Aulaire. *Ingri and Edgar Parin d'Aulaire's Book of Greek Myths.* Garden City, NY: Doubleday Books for Young Readers, 1980.

De Botton, Alain. *Religion for Atheists: A Non-Believer's Guide to the Uses of Religion.* New York: Pantheon, 2012.

———. *The Architecture of Happiness.* New York: Vintage, 2008. Kindle.

Dennett, Daniel C. *Breaking the Spell: Religion as a Natural Phenomenon.* New York and London: Penguin, 2007.

Dowd, Maureen. "Why God?" *The New York Times*, December 25, 2012.

Ehrenreich, Barbara. "The Missionary Position." The Baffler. November 2012.

Epicurus. *The Essential Epicurus*. Translated by Eugene M. O'Connor. Buffalo, NY: Great Books in Philosophy, 1993.

Epstein, Greg. *Good without God: What a Billion Nonreligious People Do Believe*. New York: Harper Collins, 2010.

Gorman, Amanda. *The Hill We Climb*. New York: Viking, 2021.

Green, Ruth Hurmence. *A Born Again Skeptic's Guide to the Bible*. Madison, WI: Freedom From Religion Foundation, 1999 (1979).

Harris, Sam. *Lying*. Opelousas, LA: Four Elephants Press, 2013.

Holmes, Pete. *Dirty Clean*. HBO, 2018.

Humanists International. "Freedom of Thought Report." Accessed October 5, 2022.

Jacoby, Susan. "The Blessings of Atheism." *The New York Times*, January 5, 2013.

Jillette, Penn. *God, No!* New York: Simon and Schuster, 2011.

Keller, Timothy. *On Death*. New York: Penguin, 2020.

Kroeger, Brooke. *Passing: When People Can't Be Who They Are*. New York: Public Affairs, 2003.

Kuile, Casper ter. *The Power of Ritual: Turning Everyday Activities into Soulful Practices*. New York: HarperCollins, 2020.

Lamott, Anne. *Help, Thanks, Wow: The Three Essential Prayers*. New York: Penguin, 2012.

Lewis, C. S. *Letters to Malcolm: Chiefly on Prayer*. New York: Harcourt, Brace & World, 1964.

Lewis, Michael. "The Art of the Untold Story." Season 2, Episode 3 of "Against the Rules with Michael Lewis." Podcast. Pushkin Industries, April 5, 2022.

Martin, James. *Learning to Pray: A Guide for Everyone*. San Francisco: HarperOne, 2021.

May, Todd. *Death*. London: Routledge, 2014.

Milk, Harvey. "That's What America Is." Presented at the San Francisco Gay Freedom Day Parade, June 25, 1978.

Mills, Claudia. "Passing: The Ethics of Pretending to Be What You Are Not." *Social Theory and Practice*, vol. 25, no. 1 (1999): 29–51.

Mitchell, Deborah. *Growing Up Godless: A Parent's Guide to Raising Kids without Religion*. New York: Sterling Ethos, 2014.

Murray, Sarah C. "The Role of Religion in Greek Sport." In A Companion to Sport and Spectacle in Greek and Roman Antiquity, edited by Paul Christesen and Donald G. Kyle, 309–319. John Wiley & Sons, 2013.

Nasr, Seyyed Hossein, ed. *The Study Quran*. San Francisco: HarperOne, 2015.

Ovid. *The Metamorphoses*. Translated by Anthony S. Kline. The Ovid Collection, University of Virginia, 2000.

Parliament of the World's Religions. "Towards A Global Ethic: An Initial Declaration," 2016.

Pieper, Josef. *In Tune with the World: A Theory of Festivity*. Translated by Richard and Clara Winston. South Bend, IN: St Augustine Press, 1999.

Poust, Mary DeTurris. *The Essential Guide to Catholic Prayer and the Mass*. New York: Alpha Books, 2011.

Pew Research Center's Religion & Public Life Project. "Religious Landscape Study," 2014.

Rich, Adrienne. "Women and Honor: Some Notes on Lying." In *The Best American Essays of the Century*, edited by Joyce Carol Oates, 412–20. Boston: Houghton Mifflin Harcourt, 2000.

Rizvi, Ali A. *The Atheist Muslim*. New York: St. Martin's Press, 2016.

Ross, Alex. "Love On the March." *The New Yorker*, November 4, 2012.

Russell, Bertrand. *Why I Am Not a Christian*. New York: Simon and Schuster, 1967.

Russell, Wendy Thomas. *Relax, It's Just God: How and Why to Talk to Your Kids about Religion When You're Not Religious*. Long Beach, CA: Brown Paper Press, 2015.

Sagan, Sasha. *For Small Creatures Such as We: Rituals for Finding Meaning in Our Unlikely World*. New York: G. P. Putnam's Sons, 2019.

Setiya, Kieran. *Midlife*. Princeton, NJ: Princeton University Press, 2017.

Shakespeare, William. *The Complete Works*. New York: Penguin Books, 1969.

TED Radio Hour. "Sandi Toksvig: Can Social Change Start with Laughter?" March 24, 2017.

Tolstoy, Leo. *The Death of Ivan Ilych*. Translated by Louise and Aylmer Maude. West Jordan City, UT: Waking Lion Press, 2006.

Van Gennep, Arnold. *The Rites of Passage*. Second Edition. Translated by Monika B. Vizedom and Gabrielle L. Caffee. Chicago: University of Chicago Press, 2019.

Vitsmun, Rebecca. Interview with TheThinkingAtheist, November 2, 2013.

Whitmarsh, Tim. *Battling the Gods: Atheism in the Ancient World*. New York: Alfred A. Knopf, 2015.

Willson, Jane Wynne. *Parenting without God: Experiences of a Humanist Mother*. Nottingham, UK: Educational Heretics Press, 1997.

Zuckerman, Phil. *Society without God: What the Least Religious Nations Can Tell Us about Contentment*. New York: NYU Press, 2010.

# ACKNOWLEDGMENTS

When I sent in the final manuscript of *We of Little Faith*, I emailed my agent, Isabelle Bleecker, and told her it would not have happened without her. Of all the stars that must align in order to get a book published, one of the most crucial is that someone believes in you and in your writing enough to make the case (over and over) that publishers should too. For me, that someone was Isabelle, and I am so grateful for her initial faith and her constant support.

Joshua Bodwell at Godine made me feel both worthy and welcome, and brought his considerable intelligence and humor to bear on discussions about what this book should be and how it should look and feel. Stephen Abbott, my editor, shaped my thinking throughout the year of writing, testing my logic, questioning my assumptions, offering his own experiences, and urging me on when my confidence flagged. This book is much more focused than it would have been without him—and more forthright too. Steve insisted that what I had to say was important, and he is a person of such thoughtfulness and integrity that I was convinced.

The *Washington Post* has given me an incredible audience, talented colleagues, and the leeway to write about everything, including the outsized place of religion in US culture. For all of that I must thank Michael Duffy, my first editor and champion at the *Post*, as well as Fred Hiatt, the late great head of opinions who hired me. Duffy encouraged me to enlarge my ambitions, both at the paper and in this book. He set my career on a different path, and I owe him a martini, possibly two.

For giving me opportunities to speak and write and exist in communities of writers, thank you to Steve Barnes, Amy Griffin, Dan Nester, Marion Roach Smith, and Leigh Stein, as well as all the remarkable women of Varied Content.

Thank you to Rebecca Vitsmun for her forthright conversation as well as her courage in doing the simplest, hardest thing: telling the truth.

For enlightening conversations about religion and God, thank you to Jill Adams, Harry Atwood, Mae Burris-Wells, John Chaplin, Chris Cohen, Leslie Cohen, Mary Hill Cole, Sandy Dovberg, Norman Dovberg, Dennis Gaffney,

Marcia Greenberg, Janet Joseph, Lee Kraus, Jessica Mann, Caitlin McCarthy, Davey Morse, David Nathanielsz, Heidi Nathanielsz, Karen Pirozzi, Kathy Ray, David Slaney, Larry Stallman, Rachelle Smith-Stallman, David Van Luven, and Isaac Wilkins.

Thank you to Anne Pirozzi for her insights on Norwegian confirmation and to Ona Nordbø-Groven at the Norwegian Humanist Association for materials and translation. Thanks also to Amy Cohen for her Greek and Latin expertise and for her thoughtful perspective on Judaism and religious affiliation.

I am deeply grateful to the first readers of my completed manuscript— Mike Larabee, Ralph Cohen, and Isabelle Bleecker—not least because the manuscript was still, in fact, incomplete in ways that I needed them to point out. I was nervous when I sent them the draft, then I reminded myself they would make it better, and they did, each according to his or her own particular genius. Jen Balderama's exquisite editorial ear made it even better, and knowing the book meant something to her gave me the courage for the final stretch. Sady Cohen, Lena Cohen-Greenberg, and Adam Greenberg all made me rethink and resee after I was no longer able to do that on my own. And what would I have done without my trusty machete, Noah Cohen-Greenberg, and his paragraph-smiting marginal scrawl: "Do we need this?"

Thank you to Judy Cohen for examining every punctuation mark with her customary exactitude. All remaining errors were reinserted without her knowledge in circumstances beyond her control. My official copyeditor, Elizabeth Blachman, not only painstakingly brought the *Chicago Manual of Style* to bear on my manuscript but also saved me many times from certain embarrassment.

Thank you to Jeff Wilkins for the immense gift of the Wilkins Residency, a week of mental space and ocean views that I will never forget. Thank you to Judy and Ralph Cohen for the peaceful, gorgeous, and well stocked Mossy Creek Retreat; you can bet I will be reapplying.

Thank you to everyone who runs, works at, and pays taxes for the libraries of the Upper Hudson Library System. Bethlehem Public Library was my second home during the writing of this book (Guilderland Public Library was my home-away-from-second-home). It gave me quiet space, good internet, a printer, all the books I needed, and, crucially, a closing time to shape my days. I apologize for always being the last patron in the building, but I did love saying "goodnight" and "see you tomorrow" to the librarians and custodians as if we were coworkers. Libraries never cease to astound me: the idea of pooling our money so everyone can share in collective cultural resources and clean bathrooms . . . they're what society should be in some utopian vision, and yet, here they are, today, in America, open from nine to nine, holding that book you wanted at the circulation desk.

My children are great readers, writers, and thinkers. They made me an atheist (see preceding book) but they also made me—and continue to make me—a better writer and a larger person. They were patient and impatient with my project in just the right amounts. They are impressed with me and unimpressed with me in just the right amounts. They are in my house and in my life just the right amount *right this minute, no changes please*.

Adam Greenberg has been the operating condition of my life since I was nineteen. We have grown up together, tested our thoughts and opinions and (now) memories against each other's, made a life together, and figured out together pretty much everything we have figured out about being grown-ups and parents. Thanking Adam for shouldering more chores this year or reading with acumen or suffering through my restless nights seems ridiculously small, like thanking the sun for drying my laundry. But, well, thank you for the laundry, Adam. Thank you for everything.

## A NOTE ABOUT THE AUTHOR

Kate Cohen is a *Washington Post* columnist who writes about the intersection of culture, family, and politics. She is the author of two previous books, *The Neppi Modona Diaries* and *A Walk Down the Aisle*. She lives on a farm in Albany, New York.

# A NOTE ON THE TYPE

*We of Little Faith* has been set in Janson, a crisp old-style typeface with a relatively high-contrast design based on surviving matrices from the 17th century Dutch Baroque period. Named for Anton Janson (1620–1687), a Leipzig-based printer and punch-cutter from the Netherlands, later scholarship asserts that the Hungarian-Transylvanian schoolmaster and punchcutter Miklós (Nicholas) Tötfalusi Kis (1650–1702) actually designed the typeface. This digital version comes from a metal version produced by Hermann Zapf in the 1950s at the Stempel Type Foundry in Germany. Berthold Wolpe's Albertus—named after the thirteenth-century German philosopher and theologian Albertus Magnus has been used for display.

*Design & Composition by Tammy Ackerman*